Dear
Dream Maker

I Don't Sleep. I Dream

Dr. Leggie L. Boone

Dear Dream Maker: I Don't Sleep. I Dream

MILTON & HUGO L.L.C.
4407 Park Ave., Suite 5
Union City, NJ 07087, USA

Website: *www. miltonandhugo.com*
Hotline: *1- 888-778-0033*
Email: *info@miltonandhugo.com*

Ordering Information:
Quantity sales. Special discounts are granted to corporations, associations, and other organizations. For more information on these discounts, please reach out to the publisher using the contact information provided above.

Library of Congress Control Number: IN-PROCESS
ISBN-13:   979-8-89285-718-5   [Paperback Edition]
                  979-8-89285-719-2   [Hardback Edition]
                  979-8-89285-720-8   [Digital Edition]

Rev. date: 10/02/2025

Dedication

This is one of those, "Finally" projects- a lifelong work, almost entirely based on my sleeping imagination. I dedicate this and all of my dreams to my Mom, my Dad, my Brother, and my Daughter. I have shared my dreams with them and several other friends, family members, and strangers over the years. I thank you for listening to me, even when they were so long that you zoned out.

I don't sleep, even though I might be snoring. I dream. My dreams are active and tiring, but I'm glad to have these stories and odd happenings to add to my days. I thank God for my dreams and pray that someone might find something in these pages that they find funny, interesting, or weird enough to re-read and share.

Table of Contents

Preface

It's Another New Day

At one point in time, I would have loved to hear someone say that he or she read my book and it changed his or her life. That was even before beginning the writing process, or rather attempting to reach my goals and facing the challenge to write my thoughts and stories for others to read. Now, I want others to know that writing has changed my life. I have written in journals and diaries for most of my days, describing my feelings and dreams, but I only wrote for myself. Then I was asked, "Who would want to read this?"

The only answer I could find was, "Someone who has gone through the same situations or knows someone going through them." I believe that cliché "misery loves company" stands true. However, I am no longer continuously miserable and want to share my moments of peace and my joy. Life is full of surprises that change your path and experiences to learn from, just so that we can share them with others.

I decided to focus on the three dearest pieces of my life: my faith in God, my family, and my dreams. These three are what have held me together even when I did not realize it. I have prayed many times and have been continually blessed. As a teenager, I prayed for patience and for guidance and know they are now a part of my character. As a young adult, I prayed for particular jobs, like working with animals. God presented them to me. I prayed for positive friends and He blessed me. I even prayed for a dog to have a loving spirit in the house when times were stressful for me. God gave me four puppies at once. There have been many other blessings He has provided for my family and me, so I know He answers prayers.

My family has been encouraging and supportive with everyone they meet, which has shaped my perspective of strangers. One internet friend once wrote a poem for me and it started, "Strangers are friends we have yet to meet." My family has an uncommon closeness that draws others into our fold. It's a wonderful thing to know your family and to see their different personalities come together in worship and praise, in times of need and distress, and in times of accomplishments and celebrations. My elders have opened their doors to provide sound advice and to share their stories with me and anyone interested in investing the time with them. There is so much history in each of us and it's an amazing journey to allow the mind to travel as memories are voiced.

My dreams incorporate my goals, but also reflect a subconscious wandering of my spirit. I have traveled to distant countries and experienced different eras in time in my nightly head trips. Describing them as a whole is difficult because I cannot identify what triggers most of my dreams. I can only record them and attempt to find some meaning or develop the story ignited into something interesting or magical. The characters and general scenarios of dreams often come from daily living experiences but the situations that develop in my dreams have been intricately colorful, detailed and complete with minimal connection to my most recent lived moments. It has been as if I am in a film, acting out my part or sometimes narrating.

Yes, I babble, and my train of thought derails at times…

While working in Winter Haven, Florida, I came up with a phrase to remind me that friendship takes time and that the potential for repeating private conversations is immense, especially when the relationship has not had time to marinate. The letters DTAS became my reminder: Don't Tell Anyone Shit. When asked what those letters taped to my computer monitor meant, I would change them a little and say, "Don't Think about Self." Eventually, DTAS came to represent Dream to Achieve Success.

Dream Trips Affect Sleep, yet another DTAS, refers to multiple borders and even a few dimensions crossed when visiting places I have never been and often interacting with people I have never personally seen. Movie and television personalities, music artists, political figures, and famous personalities surface in several of my dreams, although I have not had the opportunity to meet any of them. I have no idea what triggers my sleeping imagination, yet the detail and even sounds are clear, vivid and long-lasting. I was evaluated for sleep apnea by having a sleep test in 2006. The results of trying to actually sleep with multiple wire attachments was in my opinion inconclusive, however, the technicians determined that I did not have sleep apnea. Counseling brought a different conclusion. The lapses in my breathing that I was clearly experiencing, according to my primary physician, may have been the starting moments or climactic situations for my dreams. A therapist I had seen suggested that I consider a psychic, to interpret some of my dreams. When I'm dreaming, my mind races, causing my body to physically respond, thereby impacting my actual rest. No true sleep for me. I don't sleep, I dream.

Leggie L. Boone, PhD

Marginalia

A coworker glanced at me writing in my notebook one day and told me that he is a *marginalian*, too. I had no idea what he meant and he could tell that from the expression on my face. He enlightened me on the creative aspects of writing, drawing, embellishing, and doodling around the written content area of a book- basically, letting my thoughts spill onto the margins of a page. I have found my people and my people have a name. I mention this because my handwritten dream journals are filled with drawings, doodles, stick figures, and written phrases or thoughts that came to memory before, during, and after I wrote the dream.

Armed with this centuries-old habit, I think it best to allow some space in my own publications to let the reader's thoughts spill over. I purposely formatted my book with spacing for my notes and drawings, but also for your notes and drawings. This is your copy to highlight, underline, and color in the O's, to note thoughts, or doodle pineapples and tornadoes. I also offer prompts for you to record or share dreams you have had, memories of subconsciously being someplace you haven't been in years, and dreams long forgotten or never forgotten. I like hearing some of the dreams that others are willing to share. I don't know what they mean, but I can guess or ponder the meanings. Even dreaming of other people and telling them about it (keeping it positive or PG) can be interesting- their interpretation is often strangely different from what you thought that dream could have meant. Enjoy the space and scribble away.

Disclaimers

For the purpose of this journal, this book, and any associated volume, my name is Tangela Renee Lagia Mason. Names of family members, friends, acquaintances, and folks I had some connection with in any way have been changed. Names of public figures (actors, musicians, presidents, and so on) and businesses have not been changed, although initials may be entered in the place of the name in some cases. None of my nocturnal dreams are malicious and there is no intent for libel or slander of any individual, organization, group, or entity.

Another quick thought: I write like I speak, so there may be some grammatical inconsistencies scattered throughout. It's not that I don't know how to present wording in an appropriate manner. I just want to speak conversationally, without worrying about grammar, political correctness, and overuse of clichés or slang. I consider myself forgiven.

Dreams and Tears: The Beginning

1997

June 8

Last night, I worked on a homicide scene with Rick, my Mobile Unit shift coworker. He works the Eastern District and I work the Southwest. It was a very bloody and smelly scene- she was raped and bludgeoned and had decomposed. It was hard getting to sleep. I think I kept picturing some things at the scene that we may have been overlooking.

I'm getting married in 34 days. I'll be glad when the ceremony and reception are over. It's wearing me out. I don't seem to be able to do anything that pleases Fuller, so why try? He, my fiancée, can do whatever's left to do.

Damn, I'm broke. I want to buy some clothes so bad.

June 11

I ordered a few outfits and put some things on layaway. Yesterday, we went to get our wedding rings ordered. My finger is naked ☹. I worked for ½ day and went to York, Pennsylvania to try my gown on and have bridesmaids Serena (Fulla's sister), Phaedra (newer friend), and Hannah (seasoned friend, maid of honor) fitted. I looked good and so did they.

Can't wait ☺

June 16

Twenty-plus days until. I'm in traffic on my way to Aunt Neona's, dropping off some more pearls. I'm getting excited. She's putting my wedding broom and a few other decorations together.

So much to do it seems. Well, not really. I just have my hose and garter to buy and clothes for the trip.

June 17

I wonder if I'm ever going to be all that I can be. I think that I have the potential (hate that word) to be more- more decisive, stronger, more involved, just more. I don't mind disagreeing with Fulla. I just can't stand when my point of view seems to have no sense to it. I've been getting a lot of money from my parents. Fulla seems to bring home more than I do, and just recently he has gotten involved in making wedding choices, which makes everything that I may have chosen to do or buy before seem irrational. Back to the money- I paid for quite a few things- securing the hall (which seems too small now) and the photographer, yet Fulla wants some money back for paying down on the linen.

Then I don't go out recreationally as all. Fuller can do whatever he needs to or chooses to do when he doesn't have court (which doesn't go past 12 p.m.), so he can go out with his buddies, sleep, shop, go out to eat, make appointments, whatever. All while I'm usually working. I'm not upset really. I just feel that I have been staying home for no good reason. If I want to go out without Fulla, am I supposed to go somewhere while he's working? No. I don't really want to be out that late. But it sounds spiteful when I say I want to go out without him, even though I don't know who I would go out with.

I wish I were a different person sometimes.

June 18

If we didn't disagree about some things, we wouldn't be individuals. I was talking to God last night and I realized that I'm okay, a nice girl, and I like myself just as I am. Of course, there are a few physical things I wouldn't mind adjusting and I'm trying (not very hard yet) to be open, a little more aggressive, and yet still be open-minded to different things. I would like to make more time for fun. All work and no play, etc. I want to sing. I want to get Fulla some of the things he wants for the apartment, for the car, or for himself.

I'm somewhat interested in finding another job, going to school, taking piano lessons (once I get a piano), fixing my car, and quitting Rite Aid, my part-time secondary. Sounds like a lot but I'm sure with prayer and work, all things are possible.

After the wedding, I have two bills to pay off as soon as possible- Zales and FCNB, then I can start saving again and try harder to pay off my Visa so we can look into a home, who knows where. All I do know is that even though Fulla makes me crazy with his moods and with being right (a little more than I care to admit), I love him truly.

June 27, 7:50 a.m., at work

I've got so many things going through my mind- the other night in the bathroom, my issues, my wedding coordinator, Fulla's gift, the money to spend, children, Elayne, Jeannette, breakfast, and a few other things.

I didn't get much sleep last night. I'm still trying to decide how to wear my hair for the wedding. I think I might get the back cut. I got it done yesterday and it was okay but my tracks were showing. So I ended up rodding it. I also am considering getting braids again.

I'm now looking for some info on jumping the broom- so something can be read before we do it.

I want to write a song but I can't think of a topic or starting point.

A small part of me wants to just jump into having a child. Fulla has slipped the concept in an awful lot lately, but we're not ready. Maybe by 1999, if Jesus tarries.

I miss going to church. I want to sing.

When I was a single-digit child, maybe seven or eight years old, I had a nightmare that I still clearly remember. I was in my bedroom with its two twin beds and I dreamed that somehow, the floor was covered with worms. I hated worms- the look, the feel, their movement, and all things worm-like were sickening and scary to me. I awoke in the darkness of night and lay in bed trying to think of dry thoughts because I could feel the urge to use the bathroom. I knew that I would have to get up and walk across that worm-covered floor to get out of my room. (My child's mind didn't consider the depth of the worm layer nor if the worms were in any other part of the house. All I knew was that they covered MY bedroom floor.)

I had, thankfully, stepped out of my pink fuzzy slippers, right beside my bed. I reached down slowly, straining in the darkness to determine if I could see anything moving on the floor. I took a chance and I grabbed both slippers in one quick snatch. I shook them off over the side of the bed, in case any worms were on them. I stood on the end of my bed, assessed the distance I could jump and tossed one slipper into the middle of the floor. I decided that it would take three jumps to make it out of the room. Then, I carefully, hesitantly jumped and landed on one foot, right on the slipper. I knew I had one more slipper and once I tossed it and jumped, the third jump would put me outside the open door. I made the second jump and the third to the hallway right at the edge of my door and did a happy dance in the quiet of the sleeping house.

As I turned off the bathroom light and my eyes began to re-adjust to the darkness, I suddenly remembered that I had to get back to bed. I had to jump to my slippers again to make it to the safety of my worm-free bed. I was totally committed to this dream. I stayed in the hall for what felt like a long time but may have been a couple of minutes then decided to go for it. I could see a little of the carpeted floor by the alley light coming in through the gaps between the window blinds and the curtains. I still believed that the worms were moving on the floor. I squinted again to locate each slipper and I jumped to one then the other. I slid off of the second one and grabbed my mouth to suppress my scream. I jumped onto the bed and did another happy dance.

I pulled the covers back over me and forced my eyes to stay shut until sleep came back to me. When I awoke again, morning had come, and I pulled the blinds to see them snap and roll up, brightening the whole room. I looked at the whole floor, wondering where the worms had gone. I slowly put my feet onto the carpet, away from the bed, in case they had crawled under it. I pulled my covers up to look and saw nothing. I went to the doorway, looked back and scanned the room, just to be sure. No worms in sight. I asked my Mom later if she saw any worms in the house, to which she replied, "Not since the last time we went fishing."

Since then, I have been leery of worms- not wanting to ever touch one and giving them plenty of room if I saw one on the sidewalk. Rainy days were the worst, when the worms would be all over the place.

Although I didn't write this down after it happened, I still vividly remember my pink room, plastic panel-stuff on one wall, and pink fuzzy slippers. I remember my flannel pajama set and doing dances at least twice because I made it. I had overcome an obstacle, although imaginary.

DR. LEGGIE L. BOONE

Do you remember any of the dreams or even nightmares you had as a child?

August 10, 9:11 a.m.

Who knows why we dream what we dream? Last night I had a long gross dream. I don't know where it came from, but here goes-

I remember being inside of one of the class and lab buildings at Morgan State University, not really lost but taking the long way to get to where I was going. I had a book or notepad in my arms across my chest. The room had a radio, charger, and scanner set up.

Then I recall myself and Leona Wiley, another Crime Lab-Mobile Unit, being met by Shift Supervisor Rod Torres. Some detective called the office or wherever we were and asked if they needed to stay at the scene.

They had found a woman raped and murdered, starting to rot with maggots, underground in a ditch dug into the sidewalk. I told him what info we would need when we got there and that they or he should stay in case they find something more. We got there in separate cars and talked about ordering Chinese food from the China Wok, I think. Upon arrival, they described the scene to us and I get out my sketchpad and notepad on a clipboard. I write down everything. Leona takes out her camera and they walk us around the scene. (I drew a small sketch to show what I remember, but I lost the latent lift card I drew on.) *Then I see Rod in gloves with the body on a gurney, like the ones at the OCME (Office of the Chief Medical Examiner). I said, "Ewww! Why'd you put her on my bed?"*

I think there was a sleeping area in the office.

The body I saw first had maggots crawling and was bloody. She was dark-brown-skinned and her left arm was rotted/eaten partially away.

Then I saw a second person, I think, on the same table. She was a little lighter-skinned, had glasses on and earrings and had short hair. A baby was lying dead on the inside of her right thigh and her genital area and below her stomach was cut open. But she was alive and awake.
She got up a minute later and said, "Y'all are not doing anything else to me."

She got dressed and started to walk away. Her husband, a white guy who appeared from nowhere, introduced her as Kimberly Demox and she immediately said, "Rhymes with fox," as if they said this often.

I can't recall anymore.

Where did all of that come from?

August 23, 11:48 p.m.

I'm working right now, in between calls.

I cried this evening. I talked with my bestie Elayne for the first time in two months. She called me from the hospital this morning and yesterday (only after I wrote her sending her a gift and letting her know that I was disappointed that she didn't call me on or around the wedding date, and also to tell her I miss her). She had a boy- Paul, Jr. on the 21st. She had to have a Caesarean delivery because he was too large to make it through naturally. Anyway, I pray that I have a healthy, safe, problem-free pregnancy and delivery when we get to that point.

She told me that Paul (her husband) was getting on her nerves. One problem they may be having has to do with Paul's spiritual (or lack of) relationship with God. I thanked Fulla for that- that we both believe in God and are thankful for all our blessings and trials.

Got a crime scene call in South B-More.

0054 hours

So far tonight I have had two encounters (?).
The first- a white guy, on Washington Blvd. near the High's convenience store, told me about an assault he saw last night where 5 white boys beat up a black man and he wanted to give a witness statement. Redneck. He told me, "You sure are pretty."
Drunk as he wanted to be.

The other, an old black man on Washington Blvd. around 0015 hours near Ostend told me about a hit and run, then he told me that he loves me.
It must be my Senegalese Twists.

Fulla and I stopped by my dear friend Kama's this afternoon after a wedding. She looked tired. She said I look pretty, and we look married. I guess that's good. I've known Kama since middle school when I also met Elayne.

Back to work

0155 hours

Fulla's birthday is coming up. I think I'm going to try to get a few of his friends together to go out to Tio Pepe's for dinner Saturday night. Maybe get his friends Harold or Bishop or his cousin Rome to take him to get a massage during the day, then meet them at the restaurant. I'll have to call the place. I told Phaedra (Bishop's girlfriend) and Rome- hopefully he'll have a new girl by then. Dee (Rome's ex) is supposed to be going back to DC. I'll believe that when

I see it. Anyway, I have to decide what to get him- tennis shoes, boots, play station, sword, clothes, massage, dinner, comedy club, balloons and flowers, dinner and breakfast…

October 8

I dreamed about having a baby, actually about being pregnant. Valerie Watts (from high school) and I were walking the floor of some hospital or clinic. She delivered after a period of contractions and dialog. There were a few other people there, too.

I had a contraction and was more afraid of the pain than anything. Valerie had a girl- I saw the baby right after delivery.

I also had a dream about babysitting Donut (that's what I call Monique).

I can't remember the rest. Monique is my cousin and the daughter of Jeannette, the cousin that lived with us growing up on Kenmore Road.

October 16

Last night I dreamed about taking two drinks with Ms. Tice (my high school summer job supervisor), and walking over to an ice cream truck afterward. Setting- evening nearing sunset, the ocean in the background.

Maybe it was the cheese and wine cooler I had before bed.

Fulla is weird sometimes, especially when I'm on my period.

I'm currently working on a TV Sitcom pilot about the crime lab with Leona. This could be interesting as well as profitable in the future. *Truly wish we had acted on this.

Fulla and I may be moving to Kenmore Rd. in a couple of years, so we can save up and make a couple of investments and move to Florida in 5 to 7 years. Not a bad plan. I hope we can stick to it and come out on top.

DR. LEGGIE L. BOONE

October 17, 5:40 p.m., at work

Fulla came home from work late this morning, after 11 a.m., and no call. I got up and dressed to go for a walk. I walked to Rite Aid (my part-time job) yesterday and on the way home, stepped in dog doo-doo. I stepped in dog poop today walking by the fire station. I guess I haven't been paying attention. Today when I got back from my half-hour walk, Fulla was back and getting ready to shower. No conversation at all. I made some spaghetti and got myself ready for work. I noticed his necklace and wedding ring on the nightstand while he watched TV. My heart dropped and I couldn't help but cry a little. I know I shouldn't think the worst but what else can I think?

1:00 a.m.

I'm lonely. I wish Elayne were here. I wonder what this weekend is going to be like.

October 22

He took them off to clean them. But still…

The weekend wasn't bad. Saturday, we went to Cousin Roland's birthday party and took Fuller's mother, Ms. Cassia and the sisters, his cousin Margot, and Uncle Ronald. Aunt Sylvie was a mess, but all in all, we had a good time. April (Rome's ex) was there.

Sunday, we went to Potomac Mills with Mr. & Mrs. Carper, Fulla's father and step mother. We spent too much money, but had a nice time.

Elayne and Paul, Jr. are in town for two weeks. I went by yesterday evening. He's a big two-month-old- looks like Elayne's mother. Kalie, another high school bestie, called. She lives in Pennsylvania now. I'll write to her soon.

Today, I was mean to Jack (Miller, at work). I think the movie *Rosewood* had a deeper impact on me than I thought. I guess the stories I've heard and read as well as some of the situations I've been in have built up. Racism disgust is such a strong feeling- no matter how long you hold it in, that anger has to come out. I wrote him a note of apology, but I still feel bad.

October 24

Yesterday, I had a note in my box from Jack. Paraphrased- Thanks for the apology, but it wasn't necessary.

December 11, 7:00 a.m.

At work- I just needed to put my dream down. Maybe it was the cake and ice cream…

I dreamed about a crime- a homicide. Fulla and I were getting something from a liquor store and saw a commotion outside involving police and other cars. We saw two young black guys being grabbed and thrown down to be arrested. Apparently, one or both of them had shot and killed a man a few blocks away. It happened fast but in slow motion.

I think it was in the Northern or Northwest District. I also saw Adrienne (Fulla's cousin Maureen's daughter) wearing Minnie Mouse pajamas, and some other child. Someone was getting them ready to leave in a hurry.

I was startled when the snooze alarm went off to *"Sock it to Me."*♫

December 27, 6:50 p.m.

I had a decent Christmas. I miss my parents more than usual. I remembered saying, "I want to go home," years ago, actually from about middle school to the present. I'm ready to go. Seeing them during Thanksgiving, talking with them a few times a week, buying gifts for them, plus a few things here all reinforce my desire to "go home."

Last night, I dreamed that I had Donut in the stroller and then in the car to drive around. I only recall going to a gas station. Somehow, somewhere, I lost her. I got home and she wasn't in the car seat. I didn't remember anyone stopping me to look at her. Nothing. I was so scared at what happened, plus I didn't know how to explain it.

Then I somehow got two $20's (so I thought) from Daddy. I was telling him that he didn't have to give me any money. It turned out to be two $100's and he said, "Well, keep one and I'll keep the other."

Around late-2008, I started adding titles to my dream notes so that I could recall a little more and for a better reference system. I've gone back to my once handwritten notes, typed them, and then gave them titles. Later on, I added keywords, backgrounds, and interpretations (for a while). Interpreting my dreams can be very time-consuming, yet it's amazingly interesting. I have several resources for translating those keywords, but I don't truly understand how the pieces fit together.

For several dreams, I included a prayer. Although those prayers never stopped, recording them following the dreams became sporadic. I have had several opportunities to journal my thoughts and experiences, yet my dream stories or dream movies were much more intriguing at times. I believe the real-life roller coaster of emotional, physical, spiritual, and intellectual growth and change can be rewarding overall. But somehow...when I dream, I feel like God is showing me a personal movie that He wants someone else to see. In writing them or telling them and sometimes with my amateurish drawings, I think my audience gets to take the same trip I'm taking while in my subconscious mind. Welcome to my world.

Did you ever have any dreams about a crime, witnessed or committed?

_____
_____
_____
_____
_____
_____
_____
_____
_____
_____
_____
_____
_____

Have you ever seen babies or young children you did not know in your dream?

_____
_____
_____
_____
_____
_____
_____
_____
_____
_____
_____
_____
_____
_____

1998

What Vonda Doesn't Know

January 16, 11:45 a.m.

I meant to write my dream down yesterday. I dreamt about Cousin Vonda. *I was at her house, which had hardwood floors, and someone came to the door. I was sweeping up and stopped to open the door. It was someone named George. He was 40+, had mixed gray hair in a thick bush-like style, and not bad-looking- just okay, kind of chubby and tall. He had two (separate) dozens of roses (red and yellow, I think).*

I asked who the flowers were for. He said, "For Vonda."

I must have asked a few other questions, including if he and Vonda were considering marriage. He said that it was purely sexual.

Huh???

I think I asked if Vonda knew. He said, "No." I can't remember any more.

Keywords: Vonda, George, roses, red, yellow, sweeping, sexual.

Snakes on a Path and Sick Donut

January 17, 7:10 a.m.
Last night's dreams-
1. *Mommy and I were on some path or road with woods on both sides and we laid down on our stomachs just talking. It was dark but not nighttime dark, just heavily shaded. Suddenly, I saw three snakes*

I had my left hand in the grassy area and Mommy said, "Don't make any sudden moves. Slowly move your hand beside you, closer."

I moved it and the large gray/brown snake that was dipping its head back and forth (like it was trying to find a way around my hand) slithered by me. The other two snakes were behind me, also on my left side. Snake #2 was huge and yellowish (maybe a corn snake or albino python). It was coiled loosely with its head raised. The third was up in a bush or short tree, huge and entangled through the branches. I think it was brown with a pattern- like the reticulated pythons.

That one scared me and I woke up. Maybe it came from when I was talking to Penny (Fulla's cousin) and she mentioned snakes and dream interpretations when we were talking last night. She's having a Non-Super Bowl Party next Sunday.

2. *I remember dreaming about Donut (Monique). I must have been baby-sitting and laid her on a bed with a bottle and walked away. I came back a little while later and found vomit and milk all around her face and hair. I did the same thing twice, then cleaned her up.* {Not sure what I meant here.}

DR. LEGGIE L. BOONE

Wonder what that's all about…

Maybe because Billie on *Days of Our Lives* is pregnant. Or maybe I'm subconsciously hooked on Donut or a baby period.

I need to get a computer. I've been reading up on it and Jack Miller gave me a lot of information. I'm going to write a book to include some of my dreams and a few stories about the crime lab.

Hope I can start soon.

Keywords: path, woods, lie down, three, snakes, left hand, gray, brown, yellow, reticulated python; Donut, bottle, sick.

Greek Dream

January 18
Brief one-

> *"If somebody hurt my brother, my brother,*
> *Sigma, Alpha, Kappa, and Omega…"*
> There's more that goes with this, but I don't recall the rest.
>
> *Fulla, Bishop, me, and someone else went to a step show. It was nice. All black Greeks stepped with big numbers. The Kappas did a show with file cabinets. I don't remember the details, but everyone had on nice, bright colors and were nice to each other. I told Fulla and the others a little about each show and the Zetas rocked! The singing was the best part. I wish I could remember the songs.*

Keywords: Greek, step show, colors, file cabinets, Kappas, Fulla, Bishop, Me.

In retrospect, I would never have been able to go with this group to a step show. My demeanor would have been deflated because of the animosity towards the college experience I frequently got from Fulla.

I have had several Greek or Blue and White dreams over the years. Both the Greek and Blue and White dreams reference the Historically Black Greek letter organizations from college campuses and my affiliation with Zeta. Sometimes organizations outside of the Divine Nine sororities and fraternities appear in my dreams.

Contact Man and No Sale Today

This may be the start of my "Agent" character dreams. I also dream a lot about the house where I grew up in Baltimore. The dream house is never exactly like home was back then, but the style of the interior and exterior is the same.

Tuesday, January 20, 7:34 a.m.
Two dreams

1. *I was with a girl agent/partner and we were being chased by two men with guns. We ran into a field with a group of people who looked hypnotized but we couldn't fit in. We were wearing white net cropped shirts with white skirts and undershirts and white shoes, I think.*
    By the time we found the contact man, I was almost dead and the other girl was also near death. He gave me his keys, some papers, a wallet, and a few other things from his pockets and said (with a Russian accent), "I take of those two," who were getting closer and saw us with the contact. We both ran but not before I put my hand in animal crap on the ground next to the contact, dressed in all black, and said, "Thanks," showing him my hand, "for everything," and we both smiled.
2. *I was at home on Kenmore Rd, in a house not quite the same as 3113. The phone rang. It was 7:30 a.m. and I was already up.*
    I think this was a continuation because I recall dreaming that I took a shower and I was filthy from the glowing white stuff on the walls, visible when I turned off the light. I was going to get up early and clean it.
    Anyhow, I answered the phone and the caller said, "Who is this?"
    I asked him, "Who did you want to speak to?"
    He said something and I asked who he was.
    "Mr.? Sanders," he replied and he proceeded to try to sell some life insurance plan.
    I explained that I already have benefits and policies through my job. Then I heard a noise. I wanted to keep this man on the phone in case it was a burglar or other. So, I asked him, "Just out of curiosity, where did you get our phone number?"

He said he got it from a source called Cold Spring something. Then I heard another noise and went to the top of the steps and saw Daddy in the living room. I said, "Hi Daddy," kind of excited and told the man on the phone thanks and to have a good day and hung up.

Daddy asked if the ____ (not crib, but something else) was supposed to go with him. I said, "No, Jeannette still needs that."

There were some other pieces of furniture (baby and other) in the hall upstairs.

Side note: The shower was a large stall with the faucets on the opposite wall.

Keywords: chase, partner, two men, hypnotized group, white outfit, contact, pockets, ran, animal crap, smiled; Kenmore, shower, white, phone call, Mr. Sanders, salesman, noise, Cold Spring, stairs, Daddy, furniture.

Background: None for #1; 3113 Kenmore Road was my home address from early childhood through age ~20- lots of memories of the house, the neighbors, and the block. Jeannette is my cousin who had recently had a baby (Monique). Cold Spring (East or West) was a main road through a part of Baltimore. We lived near East Cold Spring Lane.

Four Puppies and Two Kitchens

Sunday, February 15

In my dream, *Uncle Louis (Dad's brother) came over to our house to see the four puppies. He took them outside to walk and play and they went down the hill by the steps in front of the house. I came out and walked down to the street and tried to find the spot along the median that wasn't too steep to climb down and went across to the park. We must have been new in the area because I walked around as if I was unfamiliar with the area. It was getting dark, and then I saw a hot pool, not bubbling but steamy, and I saw a few people in it. There were two white guys and one white girl. There were a few others in the park. I started to get into the pool or maybe got in all the way, and then I had trouble with my contact lens. It came out and I got up to go across the street, trying not to lose it.*

When I got to the door, I yelled or knocked for someone to answer. A girl (I don't recall who) opened the door and I went inside, cleaned the lens and put it back in. There were two kitchens- one we used and one that was yellow and white that wasn't used much. My father (not my real father, Frank) called to me to bring him something that I got from the used kitchen.

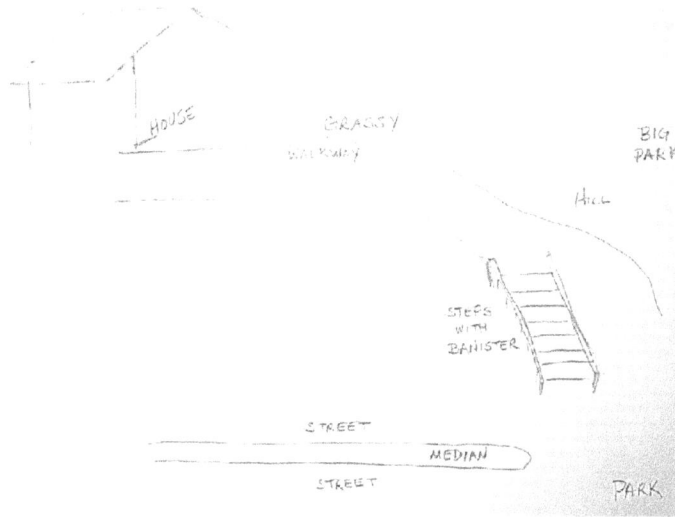

It was weird.

Keywords: Uncle Louis, Daddy, Me, four puppies, park, hill, pool, hot, three people, contact lens, kitchens, yellow, white, used

Dodged Ball

Monday, February 16

Overnight, I had a weird series of dreams. I'm not sure of the order but…

1. *I was on a date with Shawn (I think that's his name)*. I saw him at the travel agent's office Saturday with his wife. * He must have gone to Poly or Northwood or maybe Chinquapin, but I know I've seen him several times in the past. *Anyway, he and I went to some lounge and inside there was a room with steps leading to it. We were starting up the four or five steps and I hesitated. He asked what was wrong. I said something about not really wanting to be there and requested to do something else. He put his arms around me and pulled me close and said something about going to another place.*
We went to this gym-like place and there was a guy lying on the floor. Maybe he was tired from doing sit-ups. There was another guy at the end of the room who rolled a large heavy ball towards the first man. Shawn had already walked around the first guy going inside. I waited and stopped the ball, which came up to my chest, before it hit the first guy. I think he thanked me and I went to see what Shawn was doing. No more there.

Another scene was a hot tub dream- leaving that one out.

Keywords: Shawn, Me, date, familiar, lounge, hesitation, steps, gym, two men, floor, heavy ball, thanks.

Blood, Test. Flowers

Wednesday, April 1, 9:30 a.m.

I must have had at least three dreams last night.

1. *I went to a child abuse case (working 3-11) while it was still daylight. When I got there, I got some information and then saw the little boy (around 5 or 6 years old) in the back seat of a car.*

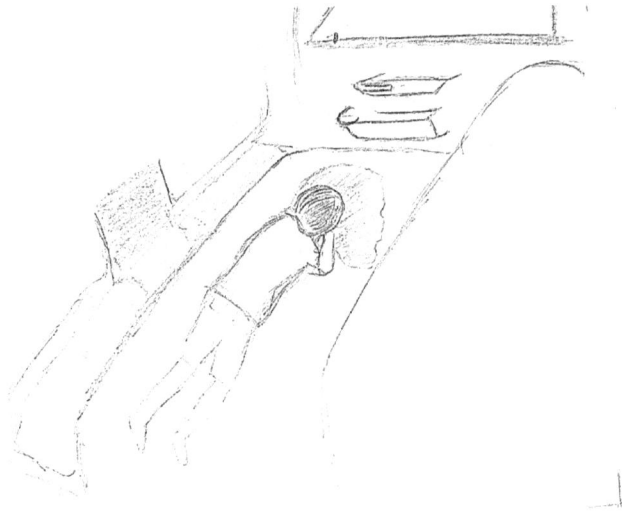

Blood was all over the seat. His head was lying in it. It didn't dawn on me to ask why he hadn't been taken to the hospital. But he was there and he sat up and showed me where he was hurt. There was a big gash on the right side of the top of his head. I was crying while I took the pictures and he was crying quietly. It was all too sad.

2. *I dreamed that Fulla told me to give Bishop some of my T-shirts. I asked, "Why? You have a whole bunch and I only have 5 or 6."*

After a while, I asked Bishop how many he needed and gave him a couple. I think it was some kind of a mind game or a test to see if I would do what Fulla told me to do.

3. *We had a whole bunch of flowers and I thought they would look pretty in vases. We had several small cup-sized vases and I broke the flowers down and put one in each cup. I recall telling Fulla not to cut them too short or we would have to put a lot of water in the vase.*

Weird, huh?

Fulla appears to be in a mood. I am, too. Kind of lonely. I talked to Elayne last night. She's moving back here soon. Uncle Derrick, another of Mom's brothers, is having surgery today for colon cancer. I pray it goes well.

Keywords: child abuse, daylight, boy, 5 or 6, blood, head wound, crying; Fuller, Bishop, t-shirts, Me, test, control, 5 or 6; flowers, vases, cut, water.

Fulla appears in several of my dreams. Over the years, I can see the control he once had over me. My dreams evolved, showing how that control slowly diminished and how my strength and self-confidence have grown in my interactions with him.

Family Matters

Sunday, April 19, 11:30 a.m.

I am in church- at Grace Baptist. I miss Rev. Owens and Min. Phillips. There's another pastor in the pulpit that was here the last time I came. I didn't care much for his delivery but I did take notes on the message.

I brought my notebook because I had a few dreams overnight. *I dreamed I had a lot more hair. It was long and below my shoulders-* I needed to get it done, but the gist of it was- I had a lot of hair. *I dreamed about Steve and Laura from Family Matters. They were young- around 13 or 14 and had put together a dance or a party for their classmates. Laura went and changed into an orange leotard, with a brown tie with white near the collar, as part of the leotard.* That was strange.

I also dreamed that I had two kids, and I looked the same- same jeans, headband, curly hairdo, almost like I look now.

Keywords: hair, long; TV characters, party, orange, leotard, Steve, Laura; two kids, I look the same

I've got to find a way to save for a computer. That seems like the only way I'm going to make this book project successful.

Pieces of Dreams are brief or incomplete dreams that I had. I didn't want to exclude them because some had what would become familiar themes and others were just odd.

Apartment Cake

April 21

> I dreamed about Cousins Scarlet and Vonda last night. They were living together in the same house. They had a big dog- a Great Dane, sitting on their back porch. They also had a cake made up like a 3-floor apartment building. It was pretty neat- in different colors. It was designed so that each apartment could be on a plate. I suggested to Scar that she give most of it to her tenants. (She owned the building.) She thought it was a good idea.

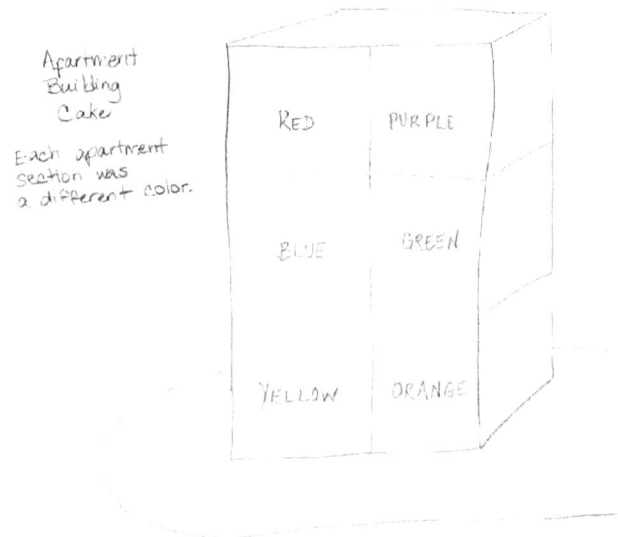

Apartment
Building
Cake

Each apartment
section was
a different color.

RED   PURPLE

BLUE   GREEN

YELLOW   ORANGE

That was odd.

Keywords: Great Dane, cake, apartment building, colorful, Vonda, Scarlet, Me

Greek Meeting

April 23

This morning, I had a blue and white dream. *There was some really big meeting being held with all Greeks- black and white, and TKE was fighting with KKE. Coppin State University Sorors were there, and we met up with some brothers we recognized. One of them looked like Timothy from Bowie State (without the beard) and another brother had locs as thick as ropes and down to the floor. He couldn't move too much or too fast because they were so heavy.*

Keywords: Greek, fight, Timothy, dreads

Moore Leggie

May 4

I dreamed I went to a B&E (breaking and entering), and the man who lived there was named Moore Leggie. I tried asking him about it but he didn't seem to understand much. He was foreign. He took me to his wife and said, "She can tell you what happened."

Get the Picture

May 11

Last night I dreamed that *I saw a big art book on the floor of this store or expo-type place where there were aisles and a center area. Before I reached it to pick it up, a man said, "Please leave that there. It's my son's."*

I stepped back and walked around some, then saw Michael Jackson sitting at a table so I went to sit beside him. We talked a little. I told him that I would be back and I walked around some more. I saw the art book again and stooped down to look at it. There were all types of drawings and pictures inside of it. I thought, maybe I can get Michael to give me his autograph on a nice picture and frame it. I chose a large picture with some flowery designs in pink, fuchsia, and black with a face in it.

I pulled it out and the man from before came up behind me and fussed some until I asked him if I could see his son to ask for the picture. He agreed, then we went to find the boy. We found him in a yard and he came over to us. The man introduced his son but I didn't understand him when he said the boy's name so

I asked the boy to say his name for me. I still didn't get it so I asked him to spell it. He was about seven or eight years old and looked like the black son from Jerry Maguire and the Cheerios commercial. He spelled N-I-M-B-R-O. Then I asked him about the picture. He and his father looked at each other and he smiled but said that he couldn't give it to me. I smiled, too, said that it was okay, and thanked him anyway.

Odd one. I guess Michael Jackson must have slipped into my dream from the CD on the entertainment center.

Keywords: Michael Jackson, art, book on the floor, father, son, picture, yard, spell, denied

Lonette and Nicolas

May 30

Dream #1: I dreamed I was eating cereal and it had a lot of raisins in it.
Dream #2: Blue and White dream
Me, Fulla, Bishop, and Phaedra went to a step show, and I saw so many old familiar faces and was hugging brothers all over the place. I even saw Jason. I sat with a few and talked some. That's all I can recall.
Dream #3: A movie
Lonette McKee was walking down a city street. She was dressed in 1920's- 1930's attire, with a hat and long coat. People were speaking to her but she ignored them or brushed them off.
There was a scene when Nicolas Cage was talking in a group of people, maybe at a club. He was also dressed for the same time period.
Then there was Lonette in a big house, locking the front screen door and then going to the back door (through nicely decorated rooms with lots of white and light colors). There was a white cat walking about. Lonette pushed a piece of furniture against the back door after locking it.
There was a voice and a knock at the front. Nicolas Cage was at the door, looking somewhat bashful. He said something about remembering this place and thought aloud that he might stop by.
There was a black and white flashback of kids playing by the swing outside of the house and laughing. Back to Lonette and Cage: she hesitates and lets him inside.

I could really do something with this. I am going to begin writing my books after the reunion.

Keywords: cereal, raisins; Fulla, Bishop, Phaedra, Me, Blue & White; Lonette McKee, Nicolas Cage; 1920's, doors, secure, flashback, childhood friends

Crossed Over to the Dark Side

June 3

I'm on the way to the vet. Last night I had a long troubling dream.

I dreamed that I was working in uniform, and went to a B&E at some store. It was evening- getting dark outside. There were a few people there- employees, maybe: one white lady met me at the door. She was moderately heavy, relatively nice- they usually all fit that description. We talked briefly and I got my regular information- the point of entry and exit, what's missing, anyone a suspect, etc.

The lady told me that she didn't believe the suspect had made it upstairs, because of the alarm. I wanted to take a look on the second floor anyway. She said, "Okay." This is where I began to lose it.

We went up the stairs and looked around a little. Then I said, "Where's the money?"

She didn't care for my tone. It surprised me, too. I became more aggressive and forceful and demanded the safe or cashbox be opened. She obliged. I took a stack of cash and papers from the top section of the box or safe, then asked the woman for her purse. She got it out from somewhere nearby and gave it to me. I must have had a gun but I don't know where I got it from. We went back downstairs. Maybe that's when a silent alarm button was pushed, but I'm not sure.

I rounded up the others into a group and then we heard police outside. I found a way out of the building and led a couple of people out to their cars. I don't know if this was before or after the police came but it was highly possible that it was after they arrived.

After apprehension, I was sitting in a room with the lady and some of the others from the store. I told her that I was sorry and that I didn't know what made me lose my mind like that. I gave her back her purse and the money and papers from the safe and we both cried a little. She told me that she knew I wasn't going to hurt them and hugged me.

Keywords: B&E, white lady, robbery, second floor, purse, escape, apprehension, remorse, cried, hugged

While pregnant and through Lana's earliest years, I know I dreamed many of my regular movie dreams, all the while living in the reality of a marriage that was far from a sweet dream. I truly believe that I was mentally abused and those scars are only visible to the ones who care to see them. I was lost. That's the only way I can describe those days, months and years. Yes, I loved the man I married.

No, I didn't recognize the red flags that should have stood out to me years later. If I had recognized the flags, I most likely would not have gotten married. At least, I hope that I would have questioned more and held onto my voice.

In the heaviest time of sorrow, I saw my brother, a true character. He sat down in front of me and asked, "Who are you?"

Pitchfork Mama

September 6, 12:51 pm (short shift change)

I dreamed between 11:30 a.m. – 12:48 pm. *Fulla and I were in the front seat, Uncle Louis was behind the driver (Fulla) and Daddy was behind me. Uncle Louis and Daddy were in the car already, before we got there. I had come over to Uncle Louis' side and he still had the door open. He was leaning inward and looked sick so I put my hand to his cheek and forehead. He said something – maybe that he would be okay. Daddy said, "Don't baby him. He's alright."*

I told him to take some of the oranges from our house when we get there.

Then Fulla and I were in the car. It was evening- kind of tornado-looking sky, semi-dark with the horizon in the background. Daddy saw her first and said, "What is your mother doing?"

We all looked over toward the house. She was coming around the side of the house, wide toward the front. She had a pitchfork with a pile of dry mulch or hay or a mixture of the two. Then she turned and was talking, leaning the pitchfork with its tips near the face of the person. Of course, our eyes followed. We all, I think, no, Fulla, Daddy and I got out and started running to the scene. When we got there, I took the pitchfork from Mom and we saw a person on their knees in a white plastic coverall suit, like the AIDS protection suit, but it didn't have pant legs or maybe it did. Sometime in all of this, Daddy also said that she had been complaining about her feet hurting and that whatever she was doing wouldn't help.

The sky was turning gray, wind was blowing a little, and there were lights like side building lights glowing. We must have been on a farm or large property. The person somehow became clearer to see because the coveralls were more like a clear plastic raincoat with a hood. It is was a white woman wearing a sleeveless dress with a red and yellow pattern. She stood up and someone must have said, "Put your hands up," and she began to raise them slowly. I noticed that the plastic had changed and I reached out to touch it. She hesitated visibly- maybe because I had the pitchfork.

I pulled the plastic and it tore away easily and revealed a tall white man, same height as the woman, heavy gut, older- early 50's, little penis- he was completely naked. We saw another person of the same look and build, naked, coming toward us. Fulla had his gun out at some point during the woman/man transformation and when the two got closer together, they came for us. Fulla shot one, but it didn't seem to affect him.

Weird dream- could be another movie.

Mr. Filbert's Mountain, Buff's Belly, and Tyler Family Shopping

September 9, 1:40 p.m., Tuesday

Sunday night I dreamed that I was in the shower and there were bubbles on the floor- a lot of bubbles. The shower had a sliding door and Haley Banks, from high school, got in the shower from the other side- she had her glasses on and braids like when I last saw her working at a shoe store, I think. We were both in the shower not saying much, facing opposite walls/shower heads. Some older white woman called out to us, asking how long we would be.

Weird, huh?

Last night, *I dreamed about a burglary scene I went to earlier.* True scene: I went to a really nasty house and met Harry Filbert, MW 56. As soon as I opened the screen door (the main door was already open) the stench hit me. It was awful. I could smell cats but I didn't see any right away. The owner/victim looked nasty, too. He had no shirt on, had those warts or bumps or moles under his arms, a big pot belly and he looked sickly. He said that he was on disability and used to work for the water department.

Anyway, the living room had bags (4-6) of trash on the floor. The ceiling in the living/dining rooms was rotted and exposed. I saw two milk jugs on the table in the kitchen- both opened and about half-filled and the table was covered with stuff- I'm not sure what, but it was piled high. I walked in with Mr. Filbert, listening and taking in my surroundings, just barely breathing while I took notes and interrupted to ask a couple of questions. I walked in as far as to the base of the stairs and at the edge of the kitchen tile at the division between the rooms, I could see a large pile, no a small mountain of cat shit. That's when I backed up and out to the door. I told Mr. Filbert that there's nothing I can do with the change on the floor and my best bet was to try the front door. So, I dusted the front screen door and made faces of bad odors at the people on the porch next door watching me. I left very shortly afterward. I stopped at the Southeast Community Police Center a couple of blocks away and talked to two officers for about a half hour and they gave me the phone number for Neighborhood Services. I called the next afternoon and spoke to an assistant director and he said that they would make arrangements to have a House Inspector investigate my complaint.

I dreamed that night that an inspector went to the house and I showed up and the trash and cat crap was gone. It was weird. The smell still lingered in the air.

September 9

Buff, my Shar Pei, is sick. I came home from work last night and he met me at the door looking pitiful and five stains of shit were on the carpet in the living room. I spent a couple hours cleaning and scrubbing then went to sleep. I woke up at ~3:45 a.m. when Fulla came in, then a couple minutes later I heard Buff squirting by the bedroom closet. I got up and cleaned it up as best I could. I woke up to Buff's whimpers at 5 something, 6:15, 8:00, 8:50, and 10 when I stayed up. Each time I took him out and each time he had diarrhea. He didn't eat anything this morning. I'm working now and about to go home to check on him.

Sometime while I slept, *I dreamed I went shopping with my mom and I saw Ava, with Anna and Ms. Mavis in the same store. It was a Penney's or Hecht's near a sale item section. I was also looking at the prices of exercise mats, for Yoga class.* I've known Ava most of my life. We became friends after high school.

Mel's Family Secret

September 10

I came in from my part-time job at Rite Aid to change so I could get to work. My stomach started hurting around 11:30 a.m. and when I was getting out of the car to come into the house, I felt really bad.

Buff had blood in his stools when I came in for lunch yesterday. I ended up scrubbing the living room floor again. Then today, I went to the bathroom, and I saw a lot of blood. My stomach hurt very badly and I cried. All the while, Fulla is on the phone talking and laughing with someone. I just cried. My body didn't hurt. It just hurt to see blood. I cried a little when I saw the blood in Buff's puddles on the carpet. On the way out the door, I kissed Fulla as usual, and I whispered that there was blood in my stools. He was still on the phone. He made a face. I mentioned that I have a doctor's appointment in the morning.

I'm scared.

There are two things that I'm very afraid of: 1) my health- I fear the worst will come of these chest/abdominal pains, and 2) that I will never have children. The pains last for different lengths of time- from seconds to maybe an hour in different areas. Sometimes in the center in the areas under my breasts or lower in the stomach- wherever, it hurts.

About children...

The time was between the years 1960 and 1965. Mel Gibson played the father, a career firefighter, with all kinds of mental, emotional, and physical battle scars. He comes home to his family after work.

Wife and two sons are in the kitchen or dining room- kind of cluttered and not too bright, the family is eating, and there's another man. The man is telling them a few stories about when he knew their father. Apparently, he knew the wife already, but not the kids very well- they were around 10-13 years old. When Mel comes in, he speaks suspiciously to the family and the man, who turns out to be his brother. The two speak mainly with their eyes. Mel says something about him not bringing anything here to endanger his family and home and watches the brother. All of a sudden, he bolts up the stairs and finds...

That's where I woke up.

Camp or Compound and Animal Quartet

October 7

This morning I dreamed:
1. *We (Fulla and I) were at some camp. At first, we were in a huge gym or flat auditorium, separated into several groups for different activities. Fulla was on a really hyped-up team and was jumping all over the place. Somewhere after this team-dividing moment, I went my own way and past Fulla's cousin Penny,*

who was walking to meet a man. She had on a skirt and they had drinks in their hands. I went past and spoke to Lorece Fenlon, from middle school. She looked nice.

I found a room with bookshelves, podiums, tables, and pianos. I found a book that looked like a hymnal that had a gold plate with several names on it- mine, I think Rome's, and others. I took that book and found a smaller room with a piano and kind of dim lighting. The book had music- words, notes, and other band stuff in it. I played a few notes.

2. **The other dream.** *I think I just walked from one to the next. I went into a house that was near or surrounded on three sides by woods. I was tired and got into the bed- a big bed in a big bedroom. I sang the Mariah Carey song "I'd Give My All" to myself and went to sleep. Sometime during the night, I saw the shadow of a person pass over me, then I fell back asleep. I guess the moonlight was shining through the windows or something or maybe someone did pass through. Later on, I woke up and saw Monique in the bed. She sat up and smiled and said, "Hi," and laid back down. I saw a frog with a white or cream-colored belly facing the door, about six feet from the left side of the bed. I also saw a Meerkat on its hind legs sitting near the corner on that same side. Near the left bottom corner of the bed was a young cougar. There was some other animal that ran past the bottom end of the bed. It resembled a hedgehog, but moved faster and its body was longer, like a mongoose. Then, each of the animals left- the fast thing, the Meerkat, then the cougar through a flap they made in the screen window. The frog seemed to have a hard time getting up to the window. I saw it using its hands (?) to pull or grab onto the curtain when it jumped.*

Prescription Diner and Long Way to the Offering Table

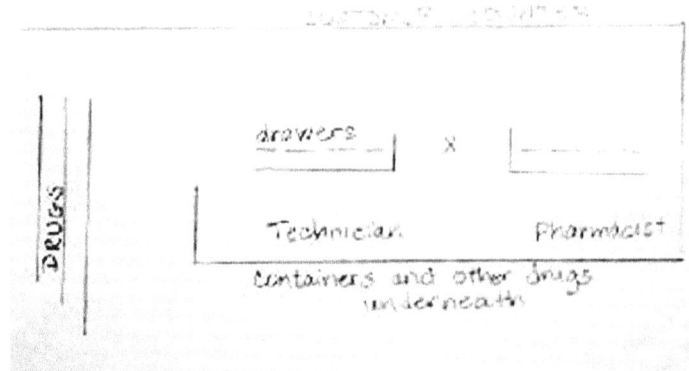

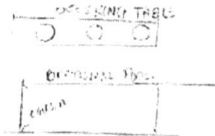

October 8

> This morning, *I dreamed that I was with Fulla, Bishop, and Phaedra. We were at some get-together and were leaving. Bishop and Phaedra were in his car (I could see the tag number) waiting on us to decide what we were going to eat. We hadn't gotten into the car yet and I told Bishop that we had hot dogs. I remember seeing me & Bishop with a short loaf of bread and when I took a piece out, he said, "That shit looks green. Nah, Sis. We're going to go get some food."*

We ended up stopping at a place that had a diner, pharmacy, books, and other gift-like items. I saw Dr. Norman and Katherine working in the pharmacy. It wasn't set up like my Rite Aid. There were counters and drawers behind them and the drugs were on either end of the long counter. The shelf in front of them wasn't as high as the vitamin shelves. Anyway, while the others walked around or ate, I said that I would go help in the pharmacy for a few minutes- 15 to be exact. Then I put some things away and filled a couple prescriptions and I came out into the store area and straightened some of the African figurines- some were cracked or chipped. Then I straightened books and saw Phaedra and Bishop. She was pregnant in the dream. I guess that's when I left.

Other dream-

I was in a hot church in Florida. I was standing and trying to help a large child or a disabled older person. We all stood to go around for offering. The pastor specifically wanted us to go around first and then drop our offerings in the basket. My row went out to the left then went around to the back. I saw Aunt Rosette kiss someone- she was a few rows behind me. Then I saw Monique standing and smiling. Then I saw Mommy standing, singing, and smiling, and then I saw Vonda naked in a small baptismal pool. She was sitting but she didn't look quite there. We (me and this unknown person) walked all the way around. I was carrying this person on my shoulder for part of the way around. We went around to the basket and I dropped in some change- a couple of quarters, dimes, and nickels, around 75 cents, and found my way back to my seat.

Mom is in Israel. She called yesterday to let us know that she's alright and enjoying herself. She went to see Jesus' tomb. I know that had to be a moving experience.

Domestic Assault and Frog Earrings

October 16

I am wearing frogs on my ears. I found them at the second-hand hat spot Mom goes to at Northeast Market. They've probably been there for a long time, but they only stood out to me the other day. The frog earrings are gold with rhinestones on their backs and are in a climbing position just like in my dream.

October 20

"To me, every rung on the ladder is important. The top is just as important as the bottom."
Jawad Abdullah

October 26

I dreamed about Rona from college last night. Some man was punching her in the face. She was outside in front of the house in a beach-like setting. I guess he was her boyfriend. They were arguing and (in slow motion, it seemed), he punched her on her left eye. I was maybe in the kitchen and saw everything from the window. I gasped and yelled to whatever man was in the house and told him, to look at what was happening to Rona. I said, "I'll get some ice," and went to the freezer. I put some ice in a towel and went outside. The man from inside had grabbed Rona's assailant and I went to Rona and helped her with the swelling/bruise and got her into the house. I think the man may have been a father, mine of some other tall, big man. My boyfriend was pretty big, too.

??? That's all I remember.

Burglary Topless

October 29

Last night, no, this morning, *I dreamed about a burglary at Aunt Neona's house. It wasn't really her house, but it was her house. Anyway, I was looking around the scene for something to dust for prints. Then I saw Jonathan and he found a window where the burglar may have entered. I started dusting some broken glass.*

I walked through the house and found Aunt Neona in her bedroom (a different bedroom) and she was helping her daughter Vonda clean up wounds on her legs. Then Aunt Neona said that she needed to change her clothes and then I saw her topless. I went down the hall and saw Cousin Teresa. She was standing and we talked a little bit. She had a young child, a baby girl, very cute, sitting on a child-sized red plastic chair. I left her and saw Scarlet, also topless walking toward me.

I really don't know where this came from.

Auntie K Playing Frogger and Scene Issues

November 28

We spent the night at the Carper's after a post-Thanksgiving dinner last night. April and Rome came- she's due next month with a baby girl and Phaedra and Bishop are having a boy.

I dreamed last night about Auntie K, my dearest great-auntie. We went to Towson (an area of Baltimore County) and I went to visit Saree and some other Sorors (sorority sisters). I asked her about a step show tape. We somehow left there and I guess we rode the bus or caught a cab and ended up walking down Woodbourne from York Rd. to The Alameda. We were headed toward 3113, I think.

We stopped at a bench on Alameda at Woodbourne to rest. Then a big truck slowly drove on The Alameda and a passenger looked over at me, smiling and saying something. I was looking to my left at him. Then, I heard the driver yell, "Watch out!"

I looked to the street and saw Auntie K smiling and walking in the street toward the truck, but somehow, she passed under the truck.

It was strange.

The other night at work, I went through so many emotions because of the scenes I attended. First, I went to an Aggravated Assault, domestic related. When I got to the block, I didn't see a police car so I requested an officer return. Then, the victim and her son came over to my car. They asked if I was here to take her husband. I asked, "Are you the victim?"

She said, "Yes," and that her husband was back. The police had left ~5 minutes ago and her husband came back in through the back door. I asked her where she was hurt and she pointed to her left eye. I called for Signal 13 and said, "5828- Please have the officer respond to the scene as quickly as possible. The suspect has returned." The dispatcher took care of it and in about three minutes, three police cars arrived. There was no struggle. When they got the husband cuffed and sitting on the grass to wait for a wagon, I went inside with the woman and her son. The boy was so sweet, ~14, and he asked me a couple of questions about the job. He stood by his mom and he kissed her after I took the pictures. When I got back to the car. The officer came over to apologize for leaving. I think I said that it turned out okay, so don't worry about it, but don't let it happen again.

Later on, I went to a shooting in the northeast. Two cousins were in the basement. One (D---) had a gun to show to J---, who hadn't seen him in ~9 months because he was in a detention center. Anyway, J--- told the police that he and the cousin went to the back door and someone shot D---, then they moved the victim to the front area of the basement. After the police talked to him some more, J--- told him the truth: the cousin had a gun to show him, and when he was putting it in the front of his pants or taking it out, it went off and exploded. The bullet apparently went in his abdomen and out his butt. They said he was stable when he went to the hospital. J--- waited with Officer Bx and me for the violent crimes detectives. There wasn't much to the scene- some blood, a casing, the victim's clothes, and the broken gun- already handled and dismantled by Officer Bx. What an idiot.

Once the detectives arrived, I did the GSR (gunshot residue swabbing) on J--- and explained a little about what was happening. He looks so sad, as he should have. Anyway, the unit at the hospital called over the radio to Officer Bx that the victim was 10-7 (expired) and that he would call 2100 (homicide unit).

J--- asked what did all that mean? Bx told him that his cousin was dead and that a homicide detective would be doing the investigation. Then the officer started talking about his overtime and missing Thanksgiving dinner, etc. Tactless bastard. My heart broke for J---. I went to get him a napkin or something then I did the GSR. The detectives were as appalled by Officer Bx as I was and told Bx and J--- not to say anything until the homicide detectives arrived.

The phone rang. The three detectives were upstairs with the victim's grandmother, and a few other people. The caller was J---'s mother, M---. Grandma called downstairs to the officer to get the phone and Bx answered the phone. M--- must have asked what was happening and Bx told her that there was a shooting, J--- was involved, no he's not hurt, she had to go downtown, yes someone was hurt, D---, sorry, but yes, he is. M--- must have asked to speak to grandma and she told grandma. Of course, we could tell that she was upset. The two detectives came downstairs and asked what happened. Bx said that he must have let it slip. VCTF (Violent Crimes Task Force) calmed grandma down, then homicide arrived. We told him the situation before he came in.

While Detective La- was in the basement, the victim's mother C--- called and told grandma that the boy was gone and to come to the hospital. Grandma got upset for real. I finished up and started my exit, sketch, etc., evidence collection, etc., to go to the hospital to GSR the victim.

The saddest part is that it was accidental and that J--- was sincere, but the worst part to me was how ignorant and tactless Bx was. What an ass. I did have a couple of other calls: a fire- stolen vehicle burned and a firefighter was staring at me the whole time. He wasn't bad- he just let me know that I've still got it. I also had B&E, armed robbery of a Royal Farm, and another shooting- very bloody. Sad Thanksgiving night in Baltimore. There were a couple of other shootings that night, too.

Sewn Up, French Braided, Owl Thingy

December 16

I dreamed about having something sewn at some store. There were two or three women and one man. One woman was helping me. We decided on a few pieces- one had measurements of 2', another 3', and the other 4'.

Then I saw them closing the store and rushing around. We all stepped out of the store, I said goodbye, and left and they went back into the store.

I saw Jason somewhere and he had a big French braid in his hair. (?)

Then I dreamed that I was pushing a stroller down a sidewalk and I saw a little creature on the grass near the top of the stairs. The creature had the body of an owl and the face of werewolf. It followed me with its head. Then, as I passed the house, I saw it out of the corner of my eye running then leaping/ diving toward me. I screamed and woke up scared of this owl thingy.

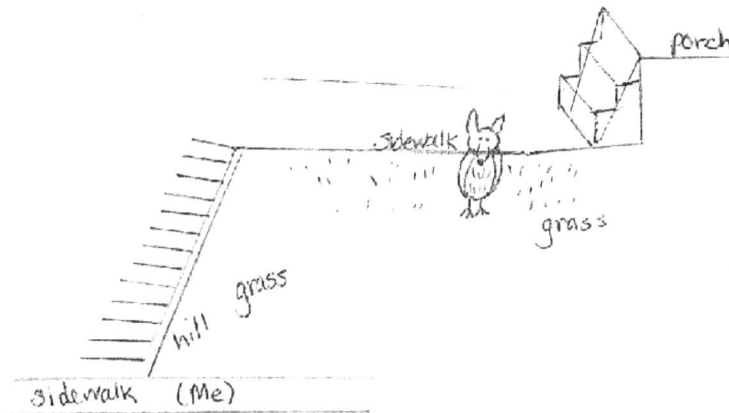

Just Notes

December 19, in the ECU (Evidence Collection Unit)
I've been meaning to write just an update.

Wednesday, my friend's mother died. She had a heart attack while driving and had an accident. I have no idea what I would do if I lost my mother, especially so suddenly.

Fulla, Jeannette, Donut, and I spent a week with my parents in Florida. The weather was pretty decent and we had a good time.

I am now 10 days late. I don't remember ever being this late. I'm afraid to get my hopes up. I keep thinking that I'm going to see something every time I go to the bathroom. Stephanie at work recently found out that she's pregnant, approximately 2 months. I hate the idea of light duty and also the idea of people being unreal and going out of their way to speak once they hear of a baby coming. It's a nice piece of news but relationships have not changed. I have a doctor's appointment on Tuesday- I'll have to sneak over while I'm working so I can at least take a pee test. I've told Stephanie and Hannah as a secret. Whatever God allows, it's OK by me.

December 24

Yesterday, I found out that I'm pregnant. I went to see my doctor after work. I was so afraid the evening before that I wouldn't be pregnant. I'm going to tell Fulla tomorrow morning as another Christmas present. I bought a cigar and a pacifier to help him guess. I wonder how he'll take it. I just got off the phone with my parents. I'll tell them in the morning, too. There's so much to do.

Have you ever had reoccurring dreams?

_____
_____
_____
_____
_____
_____
_____
_____
_____
_____
_____

Any dreams about your childhood home?

_____
_____
_____
_____
_____
_____
_____
_____
_____
_____
_____
_____

1999

Just Some More Notes...

January 2

I go to see a midwife on Tuesday. I hope she'll be able to tell me how far along I am. I'm guessing six or seven weeks, which would make my due date around August 25th. After I announced the pregnancy at Christmas dinner, Scarlet told me that from here on out, people will be saying the dumbest things to me. Miss Veronica, Fulla's step mom, pinched a nerve later that night, confirming Scarlet's words, by saying that I don't need to eat for two. I didn't eat anything while we were there and how would she know anyway when she's super small and hasn't had any children of her own. I just held my tongue, but her comment wasn't necessary. Aren't I supposed to gain some weight? I know that I'll have to watch what I eat and prepare myself for changes inside and out. Fuller will have to find a way to deal with the growth, too. I get the feeling that I'm going to get my feelings hurt from his insensitivity about weight. Anyway, I'll know what I'll have to do when the time comes. I think.

I hope the doctor has some kind of checklist and diet plan or exercise program for me to follow. I'm not sure about the order of things plus I need to buy a couple of books so I know what to expect and know what's happening to my insides. What do I want? A boy or a girl? It doesn't matter much as long as he or she is healthy, either would be fine. I want a daughter eventually so the name can be carried on. I don't know what I would name my son. We haven't talked much about it yet.

A Shark, Bump or Lump, and Notes

January 4

The night before last, I dreamed that me, Jeannette, and my mother were on a hilltop looking over a river. There were boats and people playing and swimming in the water. It was somewhat shallow 4 feet to 5 feet deep. There were also a couple of houseboats against the piers. I saw two men wading through the water as if they were looking for something, then I saw a huge shark or a small whale with a back-fin in the water really close to the men. I think I yelled down to them to watch out but we were too far away to be heard. The shark didn't attack but swam slowly around and behind them for a few minutes.

Last night, I dreamed that I was in Florida at my parent's house and my mother said she had a big bump on her leg. I think I asked to see it and she lifted her skirt and pull down the stockings and show me these huge lumps about to burst. It was nasty.

Notes:

About the pregnancy – my stomach has been queasy for a few days and my nose has become so sensitive. Some things smell so strong that they make my stomach uncomfortable. I've been getting really bad headaches – mostly a short time after I eat but sometimes just out of the blue. I hurt in the back of my head behind my right ear. I'm afraid to take anything yet. I'll wait until I speak to the doctor or midwife tomorrow.

Who Moved my Computer, Plus more notes

February 16

Last night, I dreamed that I came to work and a few of the computers were gone. I found out that they were moved to the office in a processing area when someone called requesting a set of labels for some evidence. I said that I don't think I'll be able to go back and forth down there to do DWI stuff. (We did the breath testing for DWI arrests.) *It would be convenient for some but not for others.* It was so clear.

More notes:

March 5

We are almost all the way in the house we bought. I'm ready to move out of Uncle Charles' house. Uncle Charles is Mom's brother who we were staying with to save before buying our home. Actually, I'm ready to not move into the new house. I like the new house but it's getting harder and harder to like the one I married. Fulla, Mr. Carper, and Bishop have done a good job with the wallpaper and painting. Two more rooms and the bathroom to go. I must not be much help. I guess having chest pains, headaches, and/or stomach discomfort isn't enough to keep me from moving bags, boxes, etc., wherever he wants them to go that day or pain shouldn't keep me from staying around because Phaedra and Mrs. Carper stood by their men. Per Fulla, I am inappreciative of the men who have been working so hard to get the house together and I'm not doing anything to help. He has such a fucking attitude. I truly am not liking him more and more.

I'm told constantly not to worry or to overdo it and not to get stressed but I worry, I think I overdo it, and I am stressed. That's why my chest hurts and my head throbs. Even if I wasn't pregnant and was painting alongside the fellows, I wouldn't be doing it his way, so I wouldn't be helping much or as much as he feels I should. He yelled at me and was truly nasty last night. I wanted to leave but I didn't because that would have given him more to bitch about. I stayed out of his way. He didn't look at me at all until he came down to say sorry. Big deal.

I am sorry too. I'm not the person he needs and I can't possibly handle too much more. He isn't what I need either. He complains too much, he's impatient- very. There's no room for me in his big plan. My thought of moving to Florida has been pushed aside, my opinion matters very little on house issues, and he's not supportive of my pregnancy as if he knows how I'm supposed to feel or everything there is to know about having a child. This is my very first and I want to enjoy it, make the most of it, and not be the only one to love it. Mr. Carper put me out last night after Fulla showed his shittier side. He knew that I was upset but Fulla could give a fuck. Fulla came down and helped me with my jacket. Didn't help my hurt feelings. The question is when (no longer if).

Grieving

April 23

Last night I dreamed that my grandmother died. I saw myself sitting on porch steps, crying. There was a ribbon arrangement with a cross in white and the background in red. It was very pretty. In the dream, I remembered that she's my only grandparent and I wished that I had gotten to know her better.

I had a couple of other dreams, but they weren't as bad. They were related to getting to the funeral. Cousin Cynthia came to pick me up to drive me to Virginia and I would be taking a bus to Florida.

Then Dancing

April 29

Last night I dreamed that I was in a small group with actor Will Smith, putting together music and dance moves for a video. We were in an auditorium or rec room with a stage behind us and it was dark or very dimly lit with scattered lights. The music was fast and so were the moves. Will Smith said, "Tangela, I see you doing the steps, but I want to be able to really see it." Like he wasn't convinced that I was dancing with spirit or energy.

I was wearing some really baggy pants with a loose waist. He came over to me and helped me tighten the pants and fastened them some kind away. Then he got a large key ring with several keys from the stage area and hooked them onto my pants, then we all started to dance again.

Strange.

Over the months and years between 1999 and 2003

Between 1999 and 2003, I wrote several diary entries and very few dreams. I experienced a period of heavy mental abuse, which triggered depression, anxiety, and constant fear with frequent silence, withdrawal, and bouts of crying. I didn't recognize any of this as abuse until later through therapy. Understanding what I was going through didn't fully sink in for a while. The words were spoken but they didn't register as my reality. I had been degraded and separated from family and friends. I felt alone and stuck, and I wanted to scream but worried that my fears would be met with more anger, pessimism, and complaints. I was hurting and I felt lost.

My brother, Davison, came to town and we talked. This was the heavy time I had mentioned before. He asked me directly, "Who are you?"

I didn't understand. He asked me again, two more times. I knew what he meant but I couldn't find the words to respond. Then he told me. He said, "You are not my sister. MY sister would not let someone talk down to her. MY sister would not let some man make her feel bad about herself. My sister would be strong. My sister would have said something, anything to get him straight. I want my sister back."

He got up and left me alone to think and cry a few more tears of self-pity. Eventually, I did get myself together.

This conversation and another with under two-year old Lana also stayed with me. I was sitting on the steps that led from the living room to the upper level (of our split-level house). I had been crying quietly after yet another one-sided argument with Fulla. Lana put her little hands on my cheeks and asked, "Mommy, why are you crying?"

Instantly, I snapped out of it and told her that I would not be crying anymore. (That ended up being a lie.) I told myself that I needed to be a better example of a strong woman for this little girl. So I got up, dried my tears, and made a conscious effort to be the stronger version of myself that had faded behind the cruelty of a young man.

Over this period, I secretly sought help through counseling and took on other jobs to minimize my time in the house. I felt better at times, but I dreaded being in the same space with him. He went through a few bumps himself, having torn his ACL during a foot chase, and later having a vehicle accident. Men (all men) are terrible when it comes to being patients. His physical discomfort made our situation that much worse. Somewhere during his healing, he found someone who appeared to fit his need for stimulation- physically and possibly emotionally. His on and off ring-wearing brought about a brief response of "sometimes I feel married and sometimes I don't."

After months of infidelity that was unknown to me, I learned that he had told his girlfriend that we had separated and painted an ugly picture of me as a bitchy manipulator who complained constantly.

While I was depressed and cautious around him, he was spiteful and jealous of me, for reasons I will never understand. He was jealous of my education and of any accomplishment I had achieved at work. I heard from family members who overheard his complaints amongst his coworkers in bars and clubs that, "She thinks she knows everything. Why does she get everything she wants?"

He sounded like a bully to me, instead of someone who could have been celebrating my promotion or any step I took. I felt like anything I did that was positive was a win for us and not just for me, but he didn't see it that way. He also tended to believe everything his "friends" told him about their bad relationships or baby-mama drama, thus expected me to respond accordingly. I was blatantly accused by his girlfriend of trying to drive her off the road. I had actually been with my mother on the east side of Baltimore shopping at the time the incident supposedly occurred. I even had a receipt from the store we visited that had the time and location on it to verify my statement. All I could do was shake my head. I have never felt the need to chase anyone, while driving or on foot, in anger or with any violent or fear-invoking intent. No need. If someone doesn't want me in their life, I was and still am ok with it. What God has for me is for me.

We had separated during this time and I moved out into an apartment. I didn't want much of anything from the house. The house was all about him anyway. After a burglary of my apartment, I decided to buy a house. It took a while to come out from under the storm cloud that was marriage for me, but God placed caring people in my life and I was fine. Although he had moved his coworker and his girlfriend into the house that had been ours, he still couldn't believe that I wasn't coming back to him. Buying the house truly confirmed that. We made arrangements for Lana's care in such a way as to limit our direct contact, yet he would call and talk to me as though I was still his friend. He shared a lot and wanted me to do the same, which I wouldn't. He planned to marry his new beloved and let it out that he was planning to try to get full custody of Lana, the child he barely spent time with until he and I separated. His claim was that the court would want her in a two-parent home. There would definitely be a fight on this.

While we lived out our year of separation, awaiting the time to file for divorce, Fulla and his girlfriend fought one night, ending their relationship. He had Lana there and called me to come get her. When I arrived, there were policemen there. He had put his girlfriend out, throwing her things and hitting her (unknown to the police there) and her sisters had come to get her before I got there. I asked him what had happened and he stated, "We broke up."

I asked about the police presence, and he said something about throwing her things out. Shortly afterward in the den, he told me that she was pregnant. I told him that the relationship isn't over. I told him that I was leaving. I tried to hug him but he was cold, a stiff, tall, cold block. I took Lana home and he called two times within the hour. Early the next morning, his mother called to tell me that she needed me to come to her house. I contemplated, then contacted my dear friend Elayne to watch Lana for me. When I reached Elayne's house, I decided to call his mother's house because I didn't want to walk blindly into some mess. His aunt told me that Fulla was dead. He had shot himself.

I hit the floor as if a rug had been pulled from beneath me.

So much was happening, in slow motion and at top speed. I've learned that when I am going through emotional struggles, this intense and less so, I don't remember my dreams as clearly. This was when I was forced to grow up.

2003

March 13

I haven't been writing in a while yet I know I need to. I have a very bad headache and I know that I won't get it all down, but…

A few minutes ago, El'ana asked me, "Are you scared Mommy?"

I said, "Sometimes."

She asked me again.

I said, "Yes."

She said, "You don't have to be scared," in a very sweet and comforting tone.

I love this little lady so much.

Lana's Dream

August 21, 5:30 a.m.

Why does my baby wake up so early? Guess it's because my own sleep is usually broken. Maybe.

Yesterday morning, when we were getting ready to leave for her school, *Lana told me that somebody shot her in the mouth.* I asked her to say it again so I could be sure I understood her and she repeated the same thing. She woke up coughing a little, kind of choking and said that she was sick and wanted to go to the doctor.

She told me more about her dream. *Somebody shot her in the mouth (with a water-gun). She was running and she hurt herself. Then she was crying and calling for Mommy. The police were running and driving very fast and she was scared.*

I'm praying that she doesn't have other dreams that sound like this one. I may never know how much she had seen of her Daddy's stress and illness. I'll be watchful and continue to pray.

December 12, 5:48 pm

I'm sitting, parked in front of Ava's house, kinda passing time before I drop the non-sleeping beauty over to the Carpers. Lana didn't sleep during quiet time at school, so she drifted off to sleep about 5:15 pm. I'm specifically waiting because of thoughts I've been having, pains I've been feeling, and some of the things that El'ana has said recently.

On Wednesday, The Daycare offered to keep children until 9 pm. I signed Lana up, mainly so that I could try to take care of anything- just anything without worrying about my girl. I got my hair done, stopped at the bank, and went home. I straightened up, hung pictures, set out boxes for recycling, washed dishes (in the dishwasher), and tried to clean out some of my emails. I picked Lana up at ~8:30 pm and when she got home, we went upstairs. We looked at the picture on the computer room wall. It's called "Pretty Eyes," created by Tom McKinney. I picked the print painting up at the Capitol Jazz Festival a few years ago. The little girl in it reminds me of my Jeannette. Lana looked at her expression and pose. She said, "The little girl bumped her head. She's sad. She only wants her mommy. Her mommy is dead. She only has a daddy. She needs a new mommy."

She really misses her own daddy. And, she knows he's dead and with Jesus. But, she's been using the word "dead" a lot in my opinion.

Last night was Parent Conference Night at the school where I now teach, so I had to go get Lana and come back by 5 pm. We made it and sat with the others while parents came and went. At ~7 pm, we left and I told Lana that we would stop by Ava's to see if she was home. We did and she wasn't, so Lana said, "Call her." I did and left a message. Lana asked me if Ava was dead. Scary. I told her that she might be with her friends or visiting her mommy and daddy. Lana said, "Ava is a mommy. She doesn't have a daddy."

I understood but I couldn't correct it- I guess she looks at Ava as a mother figure. Time to put on my I'm-not-disgusted-with-you face and meet a Carper.

December 23, 10:33 pm

This afternoon, after dropping off gifts at Auntie K's and taking Monique home, Lana and I went to the cemetery to take flowers to Fulla's grave. This is her first time going there and I tried to tell her that this is where daddy's body is buried and we come to the cemetery just to

DR. LEGGIE L. BOONE

say prayers and thank God for our memories. We prayed that Fulla was fine with God and let him know that we love him and miss him. Lana dutifully repeated a prayer after me and I cried for a few minutes. She asked me what was wrong and I told her that I miss her daddy. She told me, "It's okay. We'll get a new daddy."

Deep.

How does stress of any level affect your dreams? What have you dreamed about in stressful times?

_____

_____

_____

_____

_____

_____

_____

_____

_____

_____

_____

_____

_____

_____

_____

_____

_____

_____

_____

_____

_____

_____

_____

_____

_____

_____

DR. LEGGIE L. BOONE

2004

January 10, 8:04 pm

This is how my year started. Last night, Ava, her friend Enya, and I went to Club Fai's (nice atmosphere, but the music wasn't good), then to Club Kanelo's. Better music, most of the time, and more faces and outfits to behold. That mug, that top, those boots. Whoa. It was good to get out, but I must try to get a nap in beforehand next time. Below is a letter I wrote to a guy (every guy) after a night at the club.

Dear Sonny,

Thank you for the dance. It's been a while since I allowed myself to be held so close by a man, a stranger. You approached from behind and I turned to see your face. Not too bad. Just a dance, anyway, I thought. Then you came around full front still moving to the beat of some hip-hop flow the DJ was into. We held hands and did hand dance moves, with space between us. You turned me around, to my surprise. I think I was keeping up. You gently pulled me closer, and we moved together as the tunes kept playing fast, a little slower, a little faster, a not-so-decent tune, then the last song - a slow one, to end the night.

Somewhere in this series of tunes, you felt the urge to kiss my ear and neck. A moment later, I felt your tongue in that right ear. My wonderful sister-friend could see that there was some intimate expression on your part and bumped by us just to check on me. My tipsy sister. Thanks. You felt very warm and comfortable, Sonny. Good hugging size. Your face right in mine for a kiss without effort; however, I turned my face, and you get the cheek. That right cheek. Your hands move from my waist toward my big ol' butt. A no-no and I move them back with ease. Those hands slowly move up toward my breast. Another no-no. I help you move them and hug you as we slow dance to those last songs. During the not-so-decent song, you walk over to the bar in an attempt to get a drink for me and we introduce ourselves. I had been content in not knowing any more about you nor you of me, but I guess you needed more. Sonny. Tangie. We returned to the floor- bar's closed. 2:45 AM. You asked about my personal time. I tell you that I have too much take-home work for much personal time. "What do you do?" "High school science teacher." "What would your kids say if they saw you here?" "Doesn't matter. I'm still the same mellow person in the classroom." You pull me close, very close for the last dance. I feel those hands roaming and help you again. I had taken a good look at you while we briefly spoke, and I peeped in your jacket pockets as well. Just looking. About 5'8" or 9," dark skinned, clean, average build, dressed in all black, nice black leather jacket, pack of cigarettes in your right pocket, possibly a cell phone in your left pocket. Nice look- Not bad, except for the cigarettes- on the visual inspection. The question I ask myself is- Could I wake up beside this face, this person? The answer (in regard to anyone) usually comes quickly. With Sonny, the cigarette thing would bug me, and I wouldn't want anyone to change for me.

Those last moments include much pelvic motion from you. I follow some of your lead, maintaining some control of your hands and my body. The song ends. The lights come on. The DJ says goodnight. You hold on to my hand in an effort to keep me near. Your brother, Fred (I think), comes over to "meet" me. OK, then another guy and two women come. Intros all around, smiles and hi's exchanged. Then you ask, "when can I see you again?"

It's over. I'm breaking up with you. You look so confused and regrouped to ask why. I just say thank you and you'll find someone else. It will be OK. I smile and walk away. I do not look back.

You see Sonny, if you show me or attempt to demonstrate on me what could possibly occur in any personal, intimate setting out on the dance floor, then I don't want you. Sure, you feel nice- a little too nice for a few seconds here and there. You have shared more with me than I need to know, way before I even knew your name or you knew mine. You have and will share this dance with another or others. I don't want to know right away what you can do for me in the bedroom by your dance floor groove. I've been there before, too many times. On this same dance floor with men I felt a little something for while dancing. No more, Sonny. No need to exchange numbers or make plans that could ultimately lead to premature intimacy and me wondering why I didn't cut this **** off before it began. Well, I did this time.

Again, I thank you for the dance and for the refreshed feeling- the empowerment I felt in walking away, the saving of time and eventual feelings of hurt or confusion. I truly appreciate it. I wish you the best in your life- particularly in affairs of the dance floor and matters of the groin.

Blessings,
Tangie

Pilot Elayne

April 8

We're going back home tonight. We spent Spring Break in Florida. I had some interesting dreams while here. Monday night I dreamed about Fulla - it was as if we had recently met and were getting really close. It was like he was one of the fellows I had been out with this past year or two.

Tuesday night, I dreamed a few dreams. *One was about Alex, Miss Dara from The Daycare, and me. We were in a big basement cooking or doing something with food around a counter and sink. Elayne was coming over with her boys, but she was rushing and only staying for a couple of minutes. I think she was leaving the boys with us. She was flying a plane and was going to try to land it in a not-so-conspicuous area. The landing area was in the middle of a wide street with houses on each side. She landed and parked the plane and got out saying that she hoped she didn't draw too much attention and that she hoped no one called the police.*

Another dream had me driving around and talking to Kama on the cell phone. I was on some beltway or highway with very little traffic. I think I may have been going to a club somewhere.

I have got to force myself to get up and write more often.

Tuesday, we went to Busch Gardens. At times like this, I wish Fulla was here. He'd ride the coasters and have fun with Lana more than me, but he would need some other adults to ride along with him. I think Lana was disappointed since we didn't ride very much. I'll take her to Jeepers real soon.

Puzzle, Video Rumble, Wedding Parade, and Cocaine Operation

April 12

I had a couple of odd new dreams last night. *One had me finding a piece of a puzzle. It was white on both sides. Later on, I found another piece. I don't know if I was making the puzzle or just finding pieces. Even later, I decided to take a picture of Lana and have it made into a puzzle.* I just might do this.

Another dream was about a group of people- me, coworker Chris Foster, and four others - I don't recall who. We were in a classroom discussing our new living arrangements and trying to list what we would need to purchase for the house. Somehow, 11 Nachman Rd. (where I lived with Fulla) *was going to be in my hands again.*

We heard some noises and it sounded like a fight. I don't know if we went to see it on TV in a lounge or were in the house, but I think it was on a big screen. Young girls were fighting, two sisters maybe. Tossing, punching, rolling around then they heard a fight in another room. A mother and older daughter (maybe 17-20) were fighting, clothes coming apart and they were falling on the bed to the floor. Then it all looked like a home video we were all watching. When the younger girls went into the room and saw their mother and older sister fighting, the mother and sister got up and fixed themselves up trying to laugh off their tussle. Those two (mother and older sister) were playing- play fighting over clothes or makeup or something.

Yet another dream had me in a wedding as a Hostess. The wedding party moved in a line like a parade down the street. Ashley Richardson, another coworker, was in it. She was either the bride or a bridesmaid. The parade moved to a park square area set up for the wedding. The hostesses were a little ways back from the actual front part of the group. Some onlookers spoke to me and the other girls while the ceremony was underway.

I left out a dream from when we were in Florida. *I was part of some cocaine operation built into the Police Department. I was given a bag of white powder and told to separate it into smaller baggies. When I opened the package and sifted through it, it felt sandy and I saw brown and black sand mixed in with it. I got sick as I went through this stuff. I wasn't wearing gloves or a mask. I got so sick and nauseous that I vomited some thick, dark, green, nearly solid stuff. A long rope of it.* Gross.

Homicide Photo Review

June 22

On Monday (yesterday), Lana and I rested once we got to my Mom's house, and I took a nap. Summer vacation in Florida. Lana had slept in the car on the way from the Tampa Airport and she stayed in the bed watching cartoons and playing when we got to the house.

I dreamed an unusual dream- *I was called and told to come to the police department in reference to identifying and reviewing photos I took of a crime scene. It was a multi-scene case and there were four separate files that the photos were stored in within the computer. As I started to look at one folder, picture after picture, Fulla looked over my shoulder commenting. He said something like, "There's nothing there," and "You can delete that one."*

I just kept looking and I did delete one, maybe three (knowing that they could not be deleted but I gave the impression of deleting). It was strange to me that he would suggest deleting pictures. It turned out that he was under investigation- for homicide. I was scared with him over my shoulder. There were titles to each folder but I don't remember them. One of them had the number 302.

Strange

I played the number in the lottery for five days. This morning, I went in for my pre-op lab work then to Wal-Mart. I was having a bunion procedure performed on both feet. Auntie Bibi, who is actually our cousin, kept Lana so I got the lottery, stopped to get Mommy and we went to Bartow to get a Florida form for Lana's records, then to Winter Haven to go to Red Lobster. I'm nervous about the surgery but God is with me.

It's already done.

Saturday, June 26, 3:20 pm
    After Surgery…

Just waking from a Percocet nap. Lana and Mommy are sleeping still.

Yesterday, surgery was performed on both of my feet. They are each in a cast around my toes to mid-foot and wrapped in gauze and ace bandages. The operation went well according to Dr. Ward. I almost changed my mind while dealing with the anesthesiologist- Dr. Juan something. He said I kept moving during his attempts to get the IV in my wrist. That shit hurt. I was trying to stay still but I clenched when he put the needle in. I never have taken needles well. Through tears, I tried to tell him that maybe I don't need to go through this if I can't take the pain of getting the needles for anesthesia. He tried to tell me that he was giving me one drug to sedate me now and another to make me sleep through the local anesthetic for my feet for about 10-15 minutes. When I awoke, I wouldn't feel any pain while Dr. Ward did his work. I could see but I should not be able to move.

Once I started feeling the first medicine and Dr. Juan dried my tears, I felt better. I don't remember any of the surgery except for Dr. Ward telling me that it went well once he finished and to follow the instructions we had discussed when I saw him Tuesday. I vaguely remember singing "Tainted Love" when I heard it on an overhead speaker. Could be just in my head.

I was able to walk slowly in my moon boots before I left the hospital and here at my summer home. I felt some tingling, like when a body part has fallen asleep and is being awakened. Today, the pain is a little worse. Around 8:30 a.m., Dr. Ward called to check on me and I felt okay. Around 11-11:15 a.m., pains were bad- very hard to stand and walk, but I took another pill and laid down. I feel alright now but I haven't tried standing yet.

I'm debating on getting braids for the summer, or should I just continue trying to keep my hair curled. It isn't really long enough to pull off a bun.

I Hate Snakes

Monday, July 5

A nice day. Some pain in my feet- the left more than my right. The top of both feet hurt, but I've been getting along okay.

Lana saw a snake earlier today. She described it pretty good- arm's length, black and dark. We heard her screaming out front. She went out of the porch to wait on Daddy so he could start the sprinklers. Dad and Uncle Richard saw it a little while later while working in the yard. They killed it. It was about 1 ½ to 2' long (a teenager).

I wish I had been able to get out to Lana to make her feel better but my feet were up and I couldn't strap on the boots fast enough.

Later, we both took a nap and I dreamed about snakes. *In the dream, I was in a yard with Lana and Mom and I heard a noise. Then I saw a large, green snake moving very slowly across the grass from a bushy area. I called Mom and Dad. We all saw what was making it move so slowly. It was being eaten, tail end first, by a bigger green snake.* Eww.

July 6

Dear Dream Maker: Last night's dreams

One dream had me at a hair supply store that also sold perfume. I must have remembered that I needed to get a gift for Mom's birthday while I was there. The lady (a Black girl with her hair in an up do and wearing a lot of bracelets and rings) suggested a perfume called 2051.

The 2051 perfume was on the other side of the store. I asked her more about it and she said that it's new and smells really good but it costs 2051. Twenty fifty one. I'm thinking that that's cheap, but I would check it out. Janet Jackson was supposed to be working that counter but she was late or had left. I saw the perfume bottle- very big. The bottle was almost wine bottle size with an intricate top/stopper and colored glass- a shade of blue with silvery numbers. The cost of the big bottle was two thousand fifty one. Smaller bottles were $205.1 and $20.51. Cute, huh?

I guess this will be the lottery pick for the week.

Keywords: Janet Jackson, blue, silver, hair supply store, perfume, wine bottle, glass, intricate design, 2051

The Hill and the Heist

July 7

I don't know what's up with my dreams, but here goes.

One dream had me performing (singing and dancing) and I got tips. Then I went to a house on a hill and was talking to Ava on a phone. She asked where I was or vice versa- she was at the bottom of the hill with two other people, one female and one male. I told them to come on up. The girl showed me some pictures of a few people and she wanted my opinion on who she should ask out to some function she planned to attend. The pictures were cartoon-like, with some animation. The girl was Ava's friend, from Artscape last year. They left soon after that. Artscape is the annual arts festival held near the Maryland School for the Arts.

Then another dream had me with a group of people at a restaurant/lounge that looked something like the Krusty Krab (from SpongeBob Squarepants), but in real life with lower ceilings. There was a man who looked like a cross between Benny Hill and Robin Williams in a tavern-like outfit (blousy white shirt, vest and dark pants). This man was going on about some trick and a prize he had won and that he could wish for lots of money and get it. Of course, his bragging made lots of people dislike him or want to take his money from him.

A group of friends and I (band of hoods), decided to come across the top of the building and make a hole through the ceiling. There was an air mattress-type layer we could set up on top so that we could walk across it without making noise and we had (through another heist) obtained a sphere with the power of creating a path of light when lowered. When lowered, it showed a beam of light, but the light was only visible to those persons touching it.

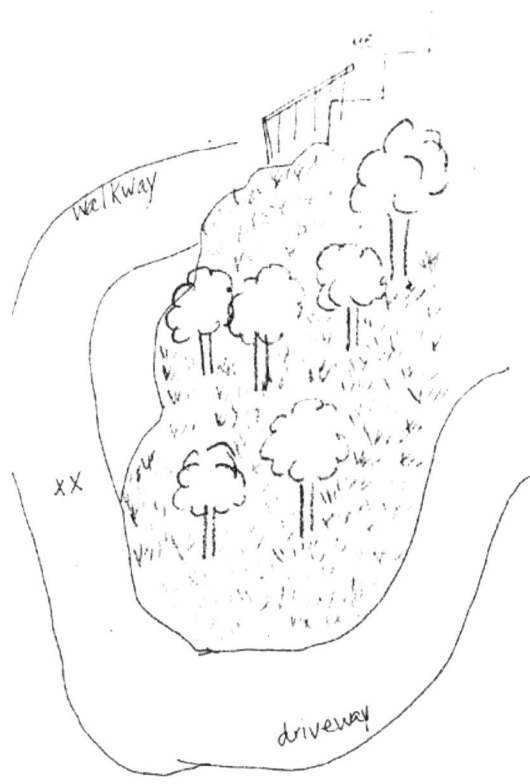

walkway

xx

driveway

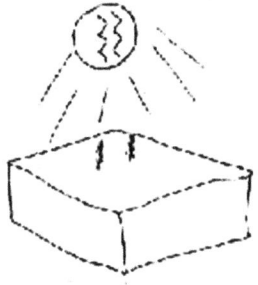

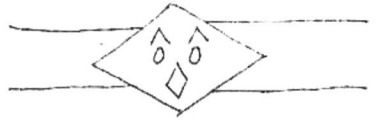

Before we got to the tavern, one agent (Beverly D'Angelo) who was a morph and something of a chameleon, eased up to one of the posts along the entry path of the tavern. She was in the shape of a mermaid when someone leaving saw her. The man glanced and turned, then looked back and just saw the post. He didn't think too long on it- just that he must have had one drink too many. Beverly had turned into another post across the top along the face of the building. The face was like a totem pole, with red features. We went through the plan of getting the thing on the roof- inflating it and making the hole to get to the money.

I don't recall whether we got the money or what happened afterwards.

Keywords: performer, Ava, pictures, hill; lounge, bragging, money, ceiling, hole, mattress, heist, sphere, light, powers, Beverly D'Angelo, chameleon, morph, drunk, totem pole, posts, red

Cinderella Wish and Note to Fulla

July 12

Dreams: *One involved a bunch of Cinderella toys and figurines. Someone gave them to me to look at and play with. They were all dressed in yellow. Somewhere along the way, I had some slippers that I had to put together- some kind of fold and bend thing. And I heard someone singing who had a voice like Nancy Wilson. I made a wish to be able to sing like that and it came true.*

Note to Fulla:
Today is the 7th anniversary of our wedding day. I would have never thought life would have put us in this place. I miss you. I did love you and love you still. Saturday, we went to breakfast at Golden Corral and went to Walgreen's afterwards. Lana wanted some sunflower seeds once she saw them on the shelf. I got them down and she told me, "I had some at my daddy's house and some at my mommy's house."

When we got back to the house, she showed the bag to my father. She asked him, "Tell me about my Daddy."

She told him, "My Daddy's at Jesus. My Daddy's sleeping. My Daddy's not coming back."

I wonder what she needed to hear from my Dad.
She told Uncle Richard, Dad's older brother, that her Daddy was at Jesus, too. She's really wanting a male figure around, regularly. All I could do at the time was cry.

Keywords: Cinderella, toys, yellow, slippers, singing, Nancy Wilson, wish

Have you dreamed about someone who has passed away? Was the person different in your dream- did they have the same personality, skills, style of dress? In your dream, did you realize they died?

Wedding Tears

July 13

I dreamed about Marvin Edwards. I always thought he was handsome. He was in a light blue, old model tuxedo and his name was Eliott. He was getting married to my friend Hannah. I'm not sure where we were but it was like a hall or convention center seminar room (a big room). There were maybe 5 or 6 other guys in the same blue suit- the groomsmen.

I talked with Eliott and he was running around nervous, making sure things were in order. He looked scared. I saw Hannah, too. She looked very pretty. I wasn't close enough for her to see me.

It dawned on me that Eliott was actually married to Diane. I wanted to ask him about that but the ceremony had begun. I went to see Diane and she was crying or had recently been crying. I woke up somewhere around here.

Keywords: Eliott, Hannah, Diane, blue, hall, wedding, pretty, crying

Lana Riding Along

July 21

I am procrastinating again. I just wanted to write down a few notes about my baby.

Yesterday, Mom got off from work early, picked me up, and we went to a couple of stores for reunion supplies, mostly. We picked up Lana in between and went to Walmart. On the way back to the house, Lana sang and talked. (She's a fun person.)

I asked her if she had taken a nap today and she said yes. Then she said, "Then the mommies and daddies come to get the kids."
> Me: After your naps?
> Lana: Yes. My daddy's at church.
> He's sleeping and he won't wake up.
> I want my daddy to come pick me up.
> He can't pick me up.
> I want my daddy.

Me: daddy's in heaven baby. It's OK to miss him.
Lana: My daddy took me skatin'. Grandma, guess what!
Me: Oh yeah?
Lana: M_____ went skatin', too. (His girlfriend)
Daddy was mean to her.
I saw her.
Mommy, you didn't see M_____.
I love my daddy.

I did well holding back the tears. I know she misses him and I wish I could make her hurting go away. I know my mom was listening and hoping I wouldn't break down. She has said, "just turn the page and move on."

I would like to move on with a new love – who knows who or when. God will be God and time will tell.

Another of Lana's Dream

August 4

When Lana woke up this morning, she smiled and told me that she had a dream. *She dreamed that she was at Walmart and got fish. She was with her sister, her new daddy, and her new mommy. She said that she paid for the fish.*

She sounded excited about having a sister and a new daddy. At first she said that I was there but then she said she had a new mommy.

She didn't want to go to school this morning.

Music Books and a Day with Prince

Wednesday, August 11

Dear Dream Maker,

I don't know what it is about me and dreams. *Monday night, I dreamed that Fulla and I were talking, sitting together. We then were with Bishop and Phaedra, talking about their upcoming wedding. They had some kind of warehouse space with a few small rooms. We were in one room and Trey came in, spoke to everyone and called Fulla and Marcus, his cousin. I left the room with Phaedra who showed me some of the gifts they had already received.*

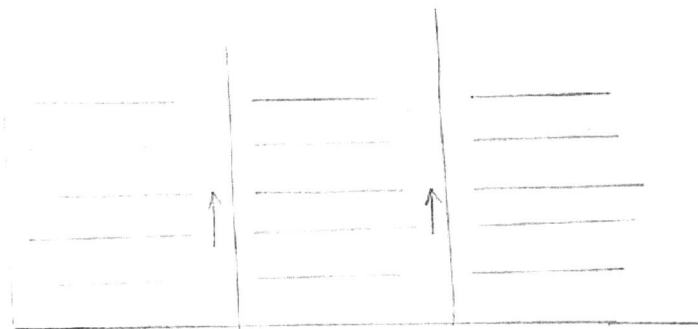

Upper shelves that rotated
big music books and other items

There was a shelf unit and the upper shelves rotated, with big music books and other items. One book had several instruments on the cover and the title "Jazz Music."

There was also a huge industrial-sized fan- almost as tall as the house. I remember thinking in the dream that my response card had "1" already written in and how was he going with me. (It didn't dawn on me until just now that he may have received his own invitation.)

Last night, I dreamed that I went to a club or lounge called Mystique. I met and talked a lot with Prince. Yes, the artist formerly known as Prince. *We were really into each other. He took me for a ride and we talked some more. Something came up about dogs. I went home- someplace different than my real home. Crazy Aunt Vinnie, my brother Davi, and someone else were there. They were about to have popcorn with a video. We spoke and I told them about meeting Prince. I got some electronic message on a handheld device that just said, "I got the Alpo." I took that to mean that Prince got the dog.*

I told Elayne about him (twice) and Prince called me to make a plan to get together later.

In between, I was driving down the street (similar to York Rd. near Woodbourne). I saw Ms. Cassia driving in front of me. She saw me in her mirror and after a couple of blocks, she pulled over and parked. She had a new house. It was very familiar. Kama (in the dream) had lived there before. She showed me around a little and I congratulated her and told her about Kama having lived there and that her biggest concern was the safety of the front door. She mentioned that she worried about that, too, and was getting it replaced. I left and later...

Met with Prince, who had a limo or some really nice car and we talked and got closer. I think we were going to see the dog.

Woke up...☹

Keywords: Fulla, Bishop, Phaedra, Trey, Marcus, wedding, shelves, rotating, music, Jazz Music, fan, gifts; Prince, Aunt Vinnie, Davi, Kama, dog, Ms. Cassia, driving, house, door.

Aardwolf Escape

August 12

Last night, I dreamed I worked at a zoo. It wasn't a zoo I had been to before. The exhibits were big and nicely arranged. I think I worked with monkeys, but I don't remember seeing any. At the end, there was a big scene to capture an aardwolf that had escaped the day before. Two others were taken out in an attempt to lure the escapee to the open. He was captured and taken away, probably to the vet to be checked.

I actually did work at the zoo for a few years before the crime scene work. Loved the animals, but the people were crazy.

August 14

We just got in from Bishop and Phaedra's wedding. Very nice. Pretty gown and lovely decor. I wish Fulla was here to share this time with them. We will never know how that would have turned out. I did good with holding back tears, remembering my own wedding, and wishing Fulla was a part of their day. I almost let loose the flood when the parents danced with Phaedra and Bishop at the reception. It made me think of Lana and her wedding. Her daddy won't be there to dance with her.

Foot Physical Therapy

September 22, 7:40 p.m.

This afternoon, I went to Physical Therapy for my feet. They're all a good group. The fellas give Lana attention and she loves going. Today, she was a little bit of a pain- whiney and loud, too much for a business. She wanted someone to play with and they were all busy today.

Around our time to go, I had trouble getting her to sit still while I got her shoes back on. Chris, one of the therapists, came over and offered to give her a ride on his back to the door after her shoes were put on. Of course, she agreed. When he got her outside and put her down, she clung to him saying, "You have to come with us. Be my daddy." She called him daddy a few times. I got her off of him and to the car where she whined while I cried.

Why are We Having a Party?

December 2

I truly should've written this down when I woke up this morning. I dreamed a rough one last night, about Fulla. Dreams feel so real when you're in them. I felt some of the old pain and fear.

A party was planned because I had returned from somewhere or maybe I had decided to get back together with Fulla. Before preparation, and his circle of friends and family's arrival, Fulla struck me with his nasty ignorant comments. It had always been his friends or family that came over.

He said "why do you always look like that? And why don't you wear something else and you always look like shit," or something like that. I listened and spoke up. "What the F#&* do you want from me? Why are you so nasty?" We actually argued.

There was also a phone call - some business called to confirm that we got two lamps that were purchased or rented for our party. I didn't know anything about them, but as I went to give the phone to Fulla, I remember wondering <u>why</u> there was a party at all and also thought that he was going to want to be intimate (even though he didn't like anything about me) and that I am not using any birth control right now.

Huge overlap of past and present life.

Why can't I think of good times in dreams? I know there weren't a whole lot of them, but I wish my dreams had a more positive focus when he does slip into them.

Flirting and Floating

December 4

I woke up a few minutes ago, lying at the edge of the bed with Lana right next to me.

Why do sleeping dreams feel so real when you're in them? *I woke up from a long dream about Brooks and me.* Brooks is a teacher and coach at my school. Exceptional on the eyes. *I had just gotten to school and was on my way to sign in, and he saw me and pulled me out to an area that was still a bit dark, some hallway. He said that he wanted his kiss. I told him that he could have anything he wanted from me. Out comes, "when am I going to get that butt?"*

I was speechless. He asked me to meet him at the office downstairs. I let him know that I'd never been anywhere except the main gym and he would have to show me. He led me through the gym, down a few stairs past a few open rooms, a small pool, then to a bigger room with two offices with blinds. There were daycare-age children with three or four adults in the open area on the floor. Brooks told me to come back down when I had a chance and he'll meet me in Miss Williams's office. I didn't know a Miss Williams in the Phys Ed department, so he pointed her out. She was sitting on the floor on her knees, reading or showing something to the kids in front of her. I asked him what time might be good. He said anytime but maybe around 10:30 a.m. or 1:00 p.m. - those were the break times or nap times for the kids, I thought. I got more kisses, not much, very soft and sweet. He seemed taller in person, and when I walked away, oops.

CARPETED

OFFICE

MATTED FLOOR

LIKE
RAQUETBALL
FLOORING

POOL

CLOSET
OR
OFFICE

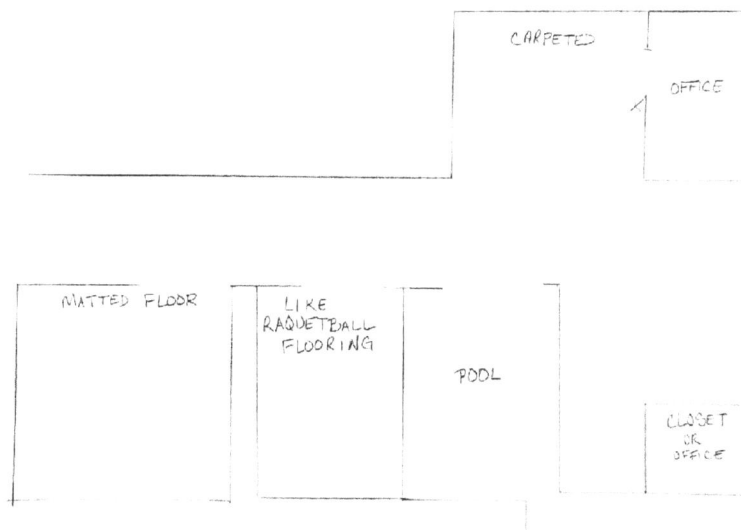

While we were talking and walking, he asked me if I had one of his students or team members. He said that the boy was interested in the military or in some way the conversation got to military talk. I mentioned my brief military experience, and for a second or two, Brooks was in fatigues. Strange.

After getting to the office area, I told him that I still needed to do a few things, sign in, get my mail, and stop along the way before homeroom and first period. And it was about 7:20 AM. That's when the kisses came in.

Then I walked away past the rooms and pool in a daze and feeling taller myself, like I wasn't walking, but floating. Felt nice. I nearly walked into the pool. Then, I walked into a matted room and turned on a light switch by bumping into it, and a bunch of little faces looked up from one area, peeking from under blankets. Once I apologized, I got back to the lobby, trying to figure out what time I could possibly slip back in to see him.

Too real. When I awoke, I thought it was true. Then reality, a little disappointment, and a good feeling too, because it was a good dream instead of a not-so-good one. I want to call Brooks but when (as I sigh) I leave messages, he doesn't call me back. That hurts. Plus, it's early. I want to tell him things, but I feel like I'm bothering him or intruding on his regular routine or life. He just wants a butt-buddy.

We went to a hula class last night, an interesting group of sweet misfits. They were all very into Hawaii and hula. I don't think I could make this class because the timing is bad. Lana slept through the whole class and it's about an hour away. There aren't any closer that I have found yet. Also, I took my braids out last night. My scalp was really itching, too much this time. I'm going to perm my hair shortly and get us ready for Lana's ballet dance class this morning.

Like an Old Movie

December 5, 7:30 am

I dreamed about actors Sidney Poitier and Lonette McKee, or people who looked like them. They were a part of some movie, traveling by foot on some dirt road walking and talking. A bad guy or small group of bandits was watching and following them. One had picked up rocks and thrown a few at them. Lonette and Sidney ran, and they came into an area with a few buildings. Lonette saw a man head up some stairs, and she threw a rock that hit him in the back of the head.

Somewhere in this dream, Sidney walked into a room where Lonette had left some music playing for him. He looked for her for a moment. Then he danced to some blues tune in a dim, small living room with a braided oval rug, wood table, and chairs. When he found Lonette, he told her that he would have liked to dance with her. All of this came before their walk. Some other stuff and dreams came up, too.

Yesterday, Lana and I went to the Science Center. It was $1-weekend there and at a few other places. We got on a couple of simulator rides that really shook me up. I saw a few people that I recognized: students Sharonne Wade and Charlotte Granger, the coach with the red locs, Diane, Marvin, and their family, and Mr. Calvert from RHS. He didn't recognize me once I did speak to him. (At least that's what he tried to portray.) He was walking outside of the restaurant area, and I gave him my number through the window. We talked for a few, and he came in once he knew that his group had found another ride. Still cute, same trifling conversation.

Have you ever dreamed about a famous person? Had you met that person before or after the dream? And, if you had the chance, would you tell that person about your dream?

What Digital Camera?

December 26, in Las Vegas

Lana and I took a nap today. I woke up sore on my left butt cheek. *I had a complex dream.*

I had driven to Randallstown High. Not the one I know. And Lana was asleep in the car. I parked on a lot on the side of the building. I could see the cemetery and Fulla's tombstone (which is actually in the ground). Mr. Carper was at the walkway and called me to ask me if Fuller's brother Mark had a digital camera so that he could get it back from him.

First question, why isn't he asking Mark for it? Second question, why wait so long to ask?

Then, Damien (Fulla's cousin), now attending RHS, said that he would like a digital camera. Mr. Carper sounded real sneaky and attitudinal about it, as if I owed him this camera. I must have dismissed the conversation. I don't remember how it ended because I didn't recall any camera among Fulla's things. I had a heavy notebook in my hands and needed to get to the building, sign in, and get back out to get the sleeping Lana. Inside, there was some event or performance going on at the steps. Vice Principal Ms. Haven was being congratulated or thanked, and several students were filling the stairs and halls. I saw

Shannon Townsend, a student, along the way, who said that the class is out in the trailer with no teacher. It was 10:30 and I was late. I was trying to avoid people at the office so that I could get back to Lana.

Ramblings and Pieces of Dreams in Vegas

December 29, 10:10 a.m., in Las Vegas

Lana woke up this morning around 6 a.m. and told me that she had a horrible dream. *She said that she was falling. One of those dreams.* Last night, after the ride, shopping, waiting on me to get a tattoo, falling asleep in the car, going to Sonic for lunch stuff, and coming in to eat- Lana got sick. She ate some fries and drank some soda. She told us that her stomach hurt and when we got upstairs, she said she had to throw up, but it wouldn't come. A little diarrhea and a few minutes later, we made it back to the bathroom just in time to throw up twice. She laid down for a while and was fine- jumping up and down on the bed in her underwear while we waited for her clothes to wash and dry.

We went out to dinner at the Tempest and after eating a few string beans and some cantaloupe, she threw up into three cups. Ewww. I don't know if she has a virus or if the morning's sausage irritated her tummy. I'll call her doctor to see if we can get in there tomorrow.

I had a dream, too, last night. *I dreamed about being a substitute for a class of bad/busy kids that looked like the School of Rock kids. They were in the street and throwing things when I pulled up in a moving truck. I had Herman Munster with me and we unloaded some things. Once kids came into the place, one kid kicked an empty can across the room. Some other boy kicked a container that was full of sugar. I spoke directly to him sternly and had him get the mess up. He tried to fight me verbally but I won and the others straightened up.*

I dreamed about Nick, from our old neighborhood, for some reason. And I had another one about owing Mom $574. The number 618 or 681 was also in the dream.

Ken Calvert is still calling pretty regularly. He would be great if...Any who, I talked with Gabriel, another former sweetheart, before we left, and (again) he said he wants to see me. It's been over a year since we've seen each other. I choose not to get my hopes up about him.

2005

From Church to Kenmore to Elementary School

January 2, 9:40 am, Sunday

I slept in Lana's bed last night. She (now 5) and Monique (almost 7) didn't leave much room for me in my bed. I woke up a while ago after dreaming this...

Ava and I went to look at a hall for a wedding reception. This place was not very big, nor bright, and was part of the lower level of a church. Pastor Crowder (?) from Uncle Charles and Aunt Sarah's church was giving us the look around. Brown paneled walls, dark-colored tile floor.

I asked him a few questions and Ava looked around a little more. I asked when he would need a deposit and he said, "today". I told him that we might not be using the place and Ava asked if she could come by tomorrow to bring her deposit. I gave her a strange look. I really didn't expect her to OK this place. I told her that if she was sure that this is what and where she wants then I would give him $50 or $100 today so she wouldn't have to come back the next day, and she agreed. The total was either $600 or $800. We waited in a lobby area for him to get a receipt book.

Somewhere else in this dream, I heard someone singing a very, pretty gospel song. I sang along and sounded really good. I think it was an updated version of "I Tried Him" (There Could Never be a Friend as Dear to Me as Jesus). A man (very much older) asked me who sang the original because we both recognized it. I think it was from one of the Gospel Music Workshops of the late 80s. I flipped through some sheet music or music books and possibly some CDs.

Then I remember being at mom and dad's house on Kenmore Rd. No one else was at home. I was supposed to be hooking up with the girls in a few hours to go out to eat, I think. Fulla came to the door and told me he was glad that I was ready. I looked dumbfounded. He took me (in what vehicle, I don't know) to Lana's school. There was a parent-teacher conference night that I didn't know about. Apparently, he had received the date and time info and didn't let me know. A weak "I'm sorry." This was just another feeble attempt to keep some control and interrupt any plans I may have had. If I hadn't been in, then he would've found some derogatory words to describe me to Lana's teacher and to Lana. She wasn't with us in the classroom at first. We sat in kindergarten chairs and talked with her teacher Ms. Wilkerson (I actually signed the tear-off for Lana's second quarter report or interim last night).

When I actually woke up and thought a little about my dreams, something led me to think of the day I went to Aunt Yvonne's salon and saw Mrs. Butler. I remember speaking and asking her about Pamela. In this exaggerated recollection, Mrs. Butler told me that Dina was doing fine also. I apologized for not asking about her but mentioned that she and I had had a falling out and I wasn't very interested in knowing how she was doing and also because Pamela looks so much like her mother, I automatically thought of her first, which was true. Weird places the mind takes you.

I should have written something on New Year's Day, but depression, laziness, and the huge mess I need to tackle have me moving at a different pace. Friday night after taking Lana to stay with Jeannette and Monique, I went to Cousin Amara's and we went to Pegasus (a club). It was different from the last time. I had been there almost a year ago or more. The music was different, more whites, Asians, and Hispanics, younger-looking crowds, and re-decorated levels. It looked OK, but I didn't feel 100% that night. I didn't look Hoochie-fly and I was worried because Lana was sick with her stomach still hurting. I was pretty, but not Club pretty. So, the men I attracted were OK to look at, but were aloof or unsure whether to even consider a second glance. I realized that people want to be with someone who looks like them. Many do. Mostly, pretty people want to be with pretty people. The men who I feel are attractive, are attractive to almost everyone, even themselves. There were some good-looking fellas in the building. Amara has the look that attracts men. I used to. I don't think that it's just my age that has affected me, but maybe my aura, one of curiosity and hesitation, and limited self-confidence. That last one makes me a fixer-upper which makes me feel less than the total package. Not downing myself, but I do need to work on that and a few other things before I think any longer about wanting someone special.

Gabriel asked me about marrying him Friday. That was a little strange. We hadn't seen each other in over a year and he has come up short too many times to count on doing what he says he will or would like to do. Plus, I think that that window has lowered tremendously, not shut but just about. I don't feel like I could handle that job now. I'm scared really. But, man, he sure is attractive.

I prayed once I got home, Saturday morning, and 2005 will be great. (Truly not written with 'great' confidence, but if I say it enough, maybe it will happen that way.)

SATT Walk, Mice & Barred Windows

January 17, 9:45am

Dreams last night and this morning were interesting. *I dreamed a few nights back about traveling to a mall. To get there we (Lana and I) went across the SATT walk to SATT City. (No idea what a SATT City walk is.) It was a long walkway attached to the side of buildings, like a sidewalk, but elevated with a little thickness of concrete underneath. The curb part had a fence, to reduce falling, I guess. When we got to the end, we went down some steps or an escalator to get to an opening like between an outdoor mall with sections.*

There were lots of people moving along the sidewalk and more areas. The walkway led to a ship, which was the mall.

And last night's dream, I was telling someone about the dream above. I also dreamed about living in a farmhouse. The rooms were big and damp, musty-like. And in one part of the dream, I was in my nightgown about to lie in a bed when I saw two mice. One at a time. The first one was light brown and white, and it ran along the wall. When I moved, it stopped, then moved along until it got to a hole in the wall.

I picked up a boot beside the bed and then saw another mouse. When I saw it heading in the same direction as the first, I threw my boot (realizing this was one of my Timberlands). I got it and blood and guts had splattered and spattered and I didn't know some had gotten on me until I felt something slimy and squishy as I moved in the night. It was all over the front of my nightgown. Ewww

In another dream, Cynthia, me, and someone else were in the same house, and because it was very cold, we were going to sleep in the same bed (a big one). We all had just laid down. Three or more helicopters came really close above the house almost all at once and there was banging at the doors. This was one of the government's security drills. Soldiers went to every window and door to check for secured locks and bars.

We rushed to make sure the windows had been locked. In one room, the soldiers outside the window were able to lift it and reminded us of the dangers of failing to check our house. ♪

The one soldier had kind of a familiar face, like Austin Owens (a student from my community college course) and I had to flirt. The song "Soldier," came out of my mouth and he smiled a little bit. We were told to have bars attached to the windows they were able to open as soon as possible. I need a 'solja'

Sometime during the next day, I had some students from forensics help me measure for putting up bars. Thomas Coles was there, but he was being his annoying, lazy self. I don't remember anymore.

January 29, ~8:00 am

I know that I had other things to write about, but I don't remember what they were.

I woke up this morning and Maya Franklin crossed my mind. Peculiar how the mind travels. That train of thought moves and switches tracks so quickly and frequently. Maya was the young lady who had a bad motorcycle accident when we were in high school. I was a freshman, and she was a senior at the time. She played tuba and I remember Mr. Andrews, the band director, asking a group of us if there was anyone interested in playing the sousaphone after she left. I volunteered. Maya wasn't exactly a friend to me, but she always spoke and wasn't evil like some upper-class women. I remember her coming back to the school a few months later to speak. I think she suffered head injuries that led to some brain damage and her legs were damaged, so she had to learn to walk again. She spoke and walked slowly. I don't remember what she said but I think it included some thank you's and a bit on safety.

February 5

Patrice, my nutty coworker and friend, Lana, and I went to the basketball game at Patapsco High last night. We sat with Mr. Henry. Mr. and Mrs. Windsor (the principal and his wife) were there, and Mr. Gundy, the football coach, too. Randallstown won 89 to 40 something. Decent game. Lana got a few minutes with her friend Mr. Windsor during halftime. A little later she told me that she wished that her friend could be her daddy. I'd heard her say that about him before. I let her know that he will always be her friend, but he can't be her daddy.

I visited with Lurena yesterday after the science technology meeting. She's doing OK since her surgery. Lurena started working at RHS the same time as me, in the same department, and we became instant friends.

I dreamed last night about Lana, Melanie Parker, Angelique Campbell, and Mommy. There was a fish tank on a stand over another fish tank. I was telling Mom good night and thought the tank on top locked crooked. So, I tried to move it, and the stand broke, and the top tank fell into the bottom tank. Big mess. Then I heard someone vomiting. It was Angelique going from a room to the bathroom, not quite making it. A few minutes later, Melanie was running and vomiting, heading to the bathroom. I checked on each and peeped in on Lana who was asleep in another room. They must've thrown up 2 to 3 times each, food poisoning, or a stomach virus. When I woke up, I had a mouth full of spit to get out. Ewww.

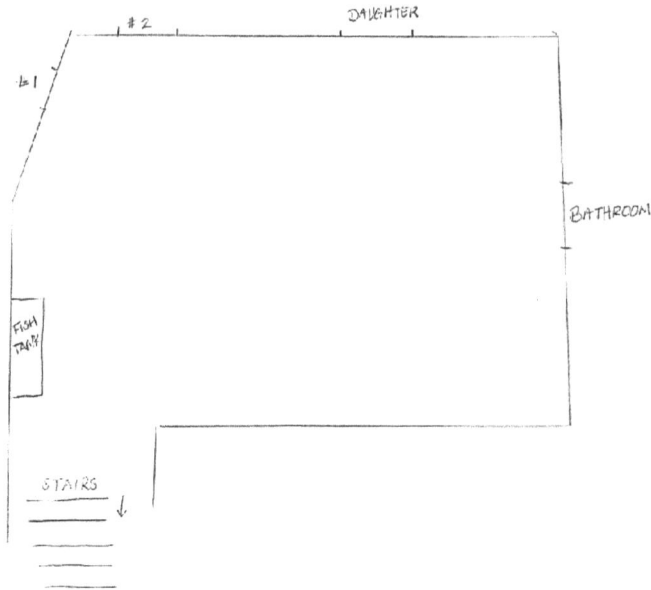

I don't know how I forgot to write about getting drunk last Saturday night. I pulled out the wine from the refrigerator. I drank about half a cup, and I was silly. I rinsed my hair and tried to wave or scrunch it and sat under the dryer. I watched some of an old movie and ate popcorn. I fell asleep for a few minutes. I laughed at myself, truly drunk, and silly. Glad that I was alone.

A note

In looking over diary entries, I recognized a pattern of relationship ups and downs. With each up, the down felt harder. With each down, I chose resilience instead of defeat. I had met some nice guys and we both determined that we weren't right for each other. There was no argument, no real drama, just understanding. I should say *understandings* since there were a few. I also realized in retrospect that I was not the only woman in a couple of these "relationships." It was and is as if fellas want to test drive the new car, keep their seasoned car, and rent a dream car all at the same time. That's a lot of gas money, but the cars don't know what the driver is doing when he's not driving them. Better still, it's that saying about wanting their cake and being able to eat it, too. Too many want cake, pie, cookies, <u>and</u> candy. I choose not to be pie. In the words of that *Chicken Run* character, "I don't want to be a Pie. I don't like gravy." She was talking about chicken pot pie, but the context is relatable for me - a locked down situation with minimal escape options and an atmosphere of unclear manipulation or control, but not quite as dangerous (in most cases). Sounds foolish, cars and pies, and it is. Anyway, I gained a stronger control of how much of my heart and energy I shared over this time. I am grateful for every person God brought into my life, for a moment or for a lifetime and any time in between.

Nosebleed, Role Play(?), and Bizarre Shopping

Friday, April 1

I got up a little while ago and waited for my visiting parents to get up so I could go get my journal from my bedroom. They are leaving to return to Florida this morning, so I need to get Lana up to say goodbye.

1. *I dreamed that Mom had a nosebleed and I told her that mine had bled recently, too.* I asked her if she did have one this morning and she said, "No," so it must have been a dream.
2. *I had another dream where Roman* (another bad relationship decision) *and I were in bed lying together just cuddling and I said, "I love you," in a whisper. He jumped and pulled away and asked, "What did you say?"*

I lied and said, "I like you." (Poor come back.) We got dressed and he put on either baseball or football clothes. I asked him if I should put on my cheerleader outfit. I got a smile and a "Later, baby." [That was unsettling.]

The room we were in was huge with a king-sized bed and another bed in it. There was a balcony above the room and my Mom must have been waiting for us to get up since she came over to the balcony and spoke.

3. *Another dream had me with three or four friends in someone's car driving to some shopping center. I went to a hair salon/cosmetics counter and asked about some products on a catalog page. Each thing I asked about had to be searched for by different people, so I waited for a few minutes and saw some people move in and out around the shop. Finally, I went back to the counter and saw Khumalo Nkosi and Shannon Townsend (getting a kiss from some man) also getting one of the things I had requested at the counter.*

Keywords: Mom, nosebleed; love, Roman, bad reaction, balcony, sports outfit, beds, Mom; friends, shopping, counter, catalog, search, Khumalo, Shannon, kiss.

Background: Khumalo and Shannon were students of mine at Randallstown. Khumalo was foreign and a little slow to understand some things and Shannon was mentally slow. I must have been really confused about "love" to have dreamt or consciously felt love for Roman. He had his positive points but in retrospect, I never believed there was "love" there.

I Saw You

Sunday, April 24, 10:42 p.m.

I'm in bed and ready to be asleep but dreading bad dreams. *Last night I dreamed about Fulla – I was meeting him to pick up or bring over Lana and he made comments about seeing me at a skating rink as if I wasn't supposed to go to the same places that he frequented. In the dream, I said to myself, "Isn't this nigga dead?" Then there was some reflection about a charge or fee for exhuming his casket.* Forgive my language.

I think this came about because I started thinking about the old pains and the anniversary of his death. I thought about the time that he came into my house to "apologize" for making me the person I was toward him. I cried some and thought about sharing some of this with Roman but decided against it.

Sunday, July 17, 10 a.m.

I just got in from church- decent message. Ask big and you'll receive big. Don't limit God. Somewhere toward the end of the message, I thought about a conversation I had with Elayne a few days ago about Fulla. Yes, I do think of him every day. The conversation included how life is different with him gone. Financially, Lana and I are better for the moment, but today it hit me (again) that money was not what was needed. We both needed his presence, his experiences, just him. Lana needs her daddy and I wish she had that much of him. So really, we're not better in any way without him. He was wrong and I was wrong for feeling that, too. Because of my own heartache and feelings of betrayal and grief, I mistook his death for a burden relieved when it wasn't that at all. It was his way to escape living and responsibility, his way to rid himself of whatever pain, self-pity, isolation, desertion, and other depressive feelings he may have felt. I miss him living and I'm sorry for having such thoughts about him no longer being alive.

I spoke with Lurena on Tuesday, July 12th (it would have been 8 years of being married). I asked for her thoughts on a relationship issue regarding Roman. I know she is right and yes, she had told me the same thing on multiple occasions in the last year +, but that day I really felt it. She is always so down-to-earth and provides some spirituality to whatever we talk about. Plus, she's fun.

Wednesday, August 24, 8:55 p.m.

I haven't talked with Brandon, my Biker Boy, today. Feels strange. I'm hoping he will enjoy himself on his trip; I don't know the time difference or his plans, so I'll just miss him for a bit.

Today, we (Science people) met at Catonsville High. I got very misplaced, basically lost, on the way. Gave myself a headache. Maybe it's PMS. This hormonal stuff gets really strange some months. I went over to RHS from there. We got our class lists- I recognized some names on my list. I said a prayer for a productive and blessed year.

I also was looking up some of my own graduation info. June 18, 2006. A Sunday. Father's Day. We can have five guests. As soon as I finish these last three projects, I will celebrate. I felt a little emotional being so much closer to my goal. I hope there is someone special to share it with me.

I've been thinking about relationships and what I want. I'm pretty solid on what I don't want but haven't been really clear on what I do want. So here goes:
-   A friendship that grows into a truly loving relationship
-   A man who has a positive relationship with God
-   A man who has a positive relationship with his mother
-   A man who is willing to be open and encourage me to be open, too
-   A man who has, as I do (home, job he likes, benefits, ya know)
-   Affection
-   Sincerity and honesty, even when it hurts
-   Courage and adventure of spirit
-   Intelligence
-   The heart of a child- willingness to try different things
-   Companionship
-   A loving spirit toward Lana
-   Devotion and loyalty

- Faithfulness
- Patience for me when I'm confused or off track
- A calm demeanor
- A playful side
- Desire to travel, yet to sometimes make me stay still
- Someone who I can repeatedly fall in love with- even when we are pissed with one another

Brief call break: Brandon just called- rainy, hurricane weather in New Orleans- expected through the weekend.
- Consistency or at least a willingness to try to be consistent
- A love of animals
- A kind and glowing demeanor
- An infectious smile
- Freedom to share and/or give himself
- A desire to learn something new
- A desire/willingness to learn something from me

I know it's a lot, but I feel that he is out there somewhere just for me and that I am all he will need in the same ways and more. Of course, my thoughts are not in order and are somewhat incomplete, but my heart and head feel that all is possible through God. I do like Brandon. Who knows, but God, how this will turn out.

December 1, 5:30 a.m.

Sometimes our old thoughts, broken pasts, and misplaced goals and dreams damage our perspective of reality. The motto or "self-promise" for 2006 is Make New Memories.

Thank you, Lord, for reminding me, through Brandon, that I do have someone willing to listen to me. I am blessed in countless ways and that alone should keep me going. My current motivational song is *Higher Ground*. Until I find the next one. My own mental push.

December 29, 10:20 pm

Mom called a little while ago. Daddy is in the hospital. He passed out briefly while he was in the store talking. No other symptoms, but they kept him and gave him a blood transfusion along with several tests. Yes, I'm worried- he's supposed to be around forever. I want to go home. I plan to go down to Florida in April for spring break.

I'm trying to financially prepare better- not by spending the $174 I spent at Staple's today, but soon and somehow, I have to get a budget in place.

I copied Lana's picture as she explained what she was writing in her diary.

Maybe if I write more, she will, too.

Lord, please take care of my dad tonight, and the next, and the next, and the next.

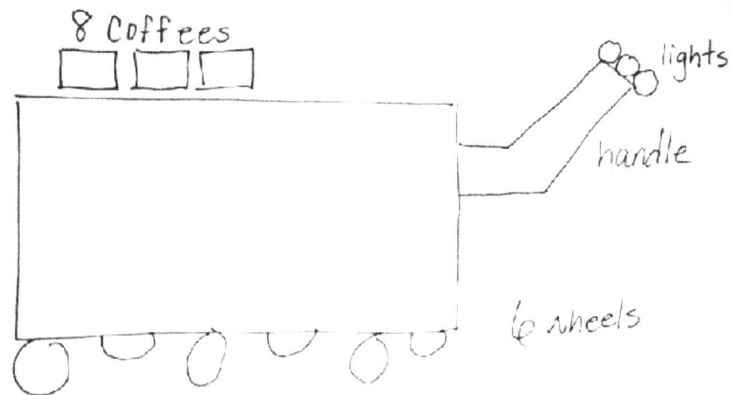

8 Coffees

lights

handle

6 wheels

copying Lana's picture as she explains what she's writing in her diary

How does stress of any level affect your dreams? What have you dreamed about in stressful times?

_____

_____

_____

_____

_____

_____

_____

_____

_____

_____

_____

_____

_____

_____

_____

_____

_____

_____

_____

_____

_____

_____

_____

_____

DR. LEGGIE L. BOONE

2006

January 12, 11:25 pm

I'm in Philadelphia with Mom at Dana's house. Dana's mom and my mom have been lifelong friends since childhood. I'm very tired but I needed to put a few things down. On Sunday, January 8th, Daddy had a stroke. I pray that God will see him and each of us through this. There has been so much support given- a true blessing. Keep him and my mom, Lord. My brother is coming up tomorrow.

January 20, 3:20 pm

Daddy passed away on Monday, January 16th. His sister Aunt Estelle and I stayed until he was gone. He had blood in his lungs from vessels that burst, and his brain had additional bleeding. His body just wore out. I am so hurt, and I miss him so much. Everything and everyone made me think of him and I just love him so much.

Lana and I are here in Florida. We got here yesterday afternoon and mom is barely sleeping. I know she has a lot to handle. Funeral arrangements, family coming in town, the phone calls, and the loss of her husband of over 42 years. The funeral is tomorrow at New Bethel Missionary Baptist- their church. He will be buried at Lakeland Memorial Gardens where Uncle Derrick's body is.

My friends have been so supportive, especially Patrice. She calls and came by and also rode with me and Lana to New Jersey and Philadelphia. Brandon has been supportive in his own way. He's sweet and it's kind of strange that he doesn't know much about a strong family, but he wants one. My Sorors have called and written with very sweet messages, too.

Faking His Death

January 23, 12:52 p.m.

Aunt Eva, another of Mom's lifelong friends, from D.C. came in town yesterday to be here with my mother.

I dreamed about Fulla last night. I dreamed that I saw him scrunched down driving a PT Cruiser, silver, like the one I rented when I got to Tampa Airport on Thursday. I followed him until he parked at a house and got out. I called the police and a few minutes later I went to the door. When I knocked, someone opened it, and I walked in. I fussed and went through the house. I found Lana's bedroom- a mustard yellow color on the walls. I got to her, and the police arrived. I needed them to see that he was alive and had faked his death. He was living with his girlfriend or wife, and their boy, and had gotten Lana while she stayed with his mother, Ms. Cassia.

Too much. I have somehow been able to picture him in the casket and I felt okay.

Keywords: Fulla, Me, same car, followed, police, entry, Lana, mustard yellow, alive, faked death, Ms. Cassia, wife, and son

Broke Scooter

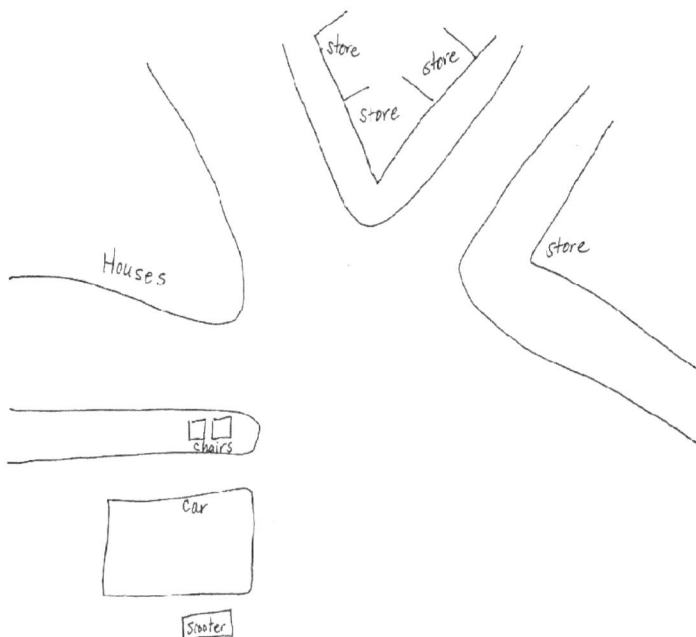

Saturday, February 18, 7:46 a.m.

    The phone woke me up- Ms. Cassia. Lana is going over there later, in a couple of hours. The dream I was having was over or ending, I think. Here goes:

My cousin Scarlet and I were out somewhere and saw an orange motorcycle/scooter and a purple/ lavender sports car I had never seen before. We stopped and asked about them. There was an Asian lady and man who said, "We run that store over there," and pointed to a corner where there were three or four stores. They said that all they needed was our licenses and, stupid-us, gave them to the lady in exchange for the keys. (Remember, it's a dream.)

I got on the scooter, got situated, and the lady ran over to me and told me to wrap the seat strap around my waist. I said, "I didn't know these had seat belts."

Once I got it started, I felt good and was doing okay. I saw Scarlet driving the sports car like she was having clutch trouble. I turned down some street that looked like Coldspring Lane by The Alameda. There were mounds of dirt and rocks as though there was construction going on. I rode near the St. George's Ave part and the scooter fell apart.

I was hitting too many rocks, I guess. I started pushing/rolling the front end back up the hill and as I was picking up the parts I could carry, I heard a phone ring from a house. It was the backyard of Kenmore and hearing the phone ring reminded me that I was late for a Sorority meeting and still needed to pick up a dessert for Diane. I saw Scarlet at the top of the block, and she asked what happened. I had a bunch of screws in my pockets and parts in my arms. I think the bike was falling apart on its own, rather than from my driving. We headed back toward the stores and the phone rang again.

A few minutes after Ms. Cassia called, Aunt Neona called. Cousin Noelle's (her daughter in-law) in the hospital. I talked to Mom some and Auntie K's number showed up. Cousin Leon, who lives with Auntie K, wanted to ask a favor but decided to call me later. Uncle Bird had surgery to remove a cancerous mass from his colon. Uncle Greg's funeral (Aunt Gina's former husband) was yesterday. Getting heavier in the Preston Family.

Keywords: Scarlet, Me, motorcycle, orange, sports car, purple, broken, old neighborhood, parts in hand, licenses, Asian lady, store, phone rang.

A Ghost Story and Fulla's House

March 8

The dream last night

I think going to the bathroom in the morning drains me of my dreams. Last night, I dreamed a ghost story. I was the main character, off and on; I'll write what I recall.

Setting: Victorian age, castle, dim passageways, no electricity, sconces with candelabras on walls; artisan made overstuffed chairs with button designs; thick wood, and pewter as common construction materials; fireplaces, arched window openings, stained glass in the inner windows, tapestries on walls, heavy drapery; moats and ponds, acres of landscaped gardens; handmade bookcases, porcelain tea cups, and more.

This young girl was standing on a ledge outside of a window that was part of a castle or a really huge, old mansion- something European. At first, I was standing with someone, and we were watching from another window that overlooked a portion of another wing of the mansion. We saw a pair of shoes on a high ledge- I don't remember what they looked like, but the shoes disappeared, and I asked the person with me (a taller person, I think a female), if they saw that. I think it was Patrice who was with me. Then, another pair of shoes appeared. They were tan colored and dressy, like a pair of low boots. The shoes slid forward one by one closer to the very edge and then disappeared. We just looked at each other.

Suddenly, a girl appeared in a third set of footwear. These were high boots, mid-calf, from some soft-looking cloth with a dark design- black and blue with a dark green, with those metal hooks to wrap the laces around. The boots had a low heel and were worn, but not ragged. The combination of colors reminded me of a big shirt that Aunt Estelle gave me. The girl stood on the ledge, outside of the iron spires that surrounded the part of the tower in our view from the window. She repeatedly looked back behind her with fear all over her face. She jumped, and we gasped and tried to scream out to her. As she was mid-air she looked at us for a second and then something stopped her in the air. It was as if she was being held upside down, just a few feet lower than the ledge from where she had leapt. She was nowhere close to the water several feet below. Even though she wore a dress with lots of layers or some cascading material, like an old-fashioned nightgown, it didn't come down over her body as she was held upside down. She looked terrified and we heard a male, dark voice saying, "You have something to do first." And, "You'll have to do this later, I'm not finished with you yet." (That was crazy.) She was turned right side up and was put back on the ledge. She was shaking and crying, and she turned, climbed over the spires, and walked the few feet to a window opening.

In another scene of the dream, I was in the same house in a room with an adult white woman, with a dark complexion like a person of Greek or Italian ethnicity, and her hair was pulled back into a loose bun. She may have been in her 30s and was dressed in the same older, 18th-century, European high-neck blouse, and long, heavy skirt fashion. She was talking with a small group (2-3 people) about something and there was a young child in the room, too. I told her I was going to get something to drink and left the room. In the first room I passed, I noticed the furniture had been moved- not drastically but as if maybe someone was looking for something and had pulled the couch and a table just a few inches over or maybe they were trying to block someone's path in the dark. This place was very dark but there was dim lighting, probably candles in a hall that allowed me to see where I was going because I didn't turn on any light switch. I got to the kitchen and had that same feeling from the other rooms I had come through. Something was off or out of place. In the kitchen, there was an old 1960s model refrigerator, with the rounded edges and long arm door handles. (Some time-period confusion going on here- no electricity, remember?) As I entered the kitchen, there was a round Formica or linoleum table with a couple of chairs, on the side farthest from the door. There were plastic cups in a package, and a few were loose, out on the table. A couple of cups were overturned and there was water on the table, but not much. I opened the refrigerator, and no light came on. I thought that was strange, but got a soda bottle out and picked up one of the cups from the table. I opened the freezer and got ice from a metal tray with a lever. I dropped a couple of ice cubes or pieces: they didn't look like ice maker-shaped pieces; more like small squares mixed with chips. There were a couple of pieces of ice melting on the floor. Then I noticed a cup on the table that had ice still in it and ice on the table melting. I drank a little soda from the cup while I was observing all of these things and felt that chill and ran back the way I came to tell the woman. When I reached her, she was in another room talking with the same group of people. She was a writer, and we were in the room where she had a display of her novels, magazines, and journals. On the shelf were large hardback books in order –it was a series of ghost stories based on one young girl, maybe a teenager, named Rose. The bookshelf was made as a display with angled shelves to show the front covers. On the top shelf, at eye level, I saw the second book cover and there was the girl who I had seen earlier out on the ledge. I know I made a face showing my confusion and I felt someone or something move past me from the side. I looked around and people were just talking and looking at the different things on the shelves. Someone asked where a few volumes of her journals and magazines were, and she said that she loaned them to Tangie for her research project and "they'll be back on the shelves as soon as she gets her work finished." She looked over at me and I nodded yes. I remember looking at the titles as if they were some message, and I saw the girl again, but I don't remember the rest of the dream. *There were drawings for this one, but I'm thinking I'll repeat this story in my next volume and include the drawings there.*

The night before, *I dreamed about Fulla. We saw each other somewhere on the street and he wanted me to come to his house for some reason. I agreed and followed him. He was in his Camaro, and I was in my Durango. He pulled up to a house that was on a street that looked like Lothian Rd., off of Woodbourne Ave. We parked and went inside, and it was dim to me, not darkly painted but dark curtains and dark furniture, and the curtains were drawn or the blinds were closed. We walked into the living room, a dining room, then through some other room, and went to another level upstairs. I left him to look around. I heard the voices of children and several people moving about the house. I had a thought, a bunch of his friends probably. Anyway, I went to a room at the back of the house and saw a lady named Mrs. Williams folding clothes and putting things away. There were brightly colored clothes, a canopy, curtains, and thin sheets or scarves hanging everywhere in mostly bright red, blue, and yellow. Her husband came out and said hello. She said they were renting from Fulla and they loved it here. I simply smiled and hugged her. I left that room and went downstairs and saw Fulla through a window outside in the back of the house talking with someone. I couldn't see the other person. I walked back towards the front to leave and saw a few children, smiled, spoke to them, and headed out the front door. I don't remember any more of that scene.*

The darkness (castles and curtains) in these dreams drains me.

House for Sale, Archie, and a Premonition

March 17, 5:40-ish a.m.

Getting ready for school but I needed to put a few things down.

Back to camp dreams last night.

Number 1. *I was selling my home, but it wasn't this house. It was the house on Nachman Rd., but on a different property. There was no pool there. An older white couple in their 50s was very interested in buying it. My real estate person and Maureen and Margot (Fulla's cousins) were there. Somewhere along the couples' tour, they asked me why I wanted to sell. I told them that I was moving South to be closer to my family in Florida, but they sensed something else. I finally told them that the man I married had died there, and I needed to get out. Maureen and Margot filled in the gaps, but their version was inaccurate in places -the room where he had died wasn't correct. No more to this one.*

A second one, I think after my nightly wake-up around 1 something, *was that I took a road trip to see Cousin Cynthia. She was seeing Archibald (a student from RHS). We (except Archie) were much younger and had no kids or husbands. The visit was just for the day and the drive wasn't really far but it looked like the trip to Frostburg- with mountains and hills. I was in the truck to leave when I couldn't find Archie. He had started walking home. In the distance, I could see him turn to look back, put his finger to his lips, and wave goodbye. I drove past him and ahead and told him to get in when he got to my truck. Maybe he thought he was taking me out of the way or just wanted time alone. I don't know.*

Yesterday, our school team went to the CSI games. It turned out well. They did a decent job and now I know what to expect next year. Last night, Brandon told me he had finally talked with his baby's mother. Rough situation. She had thought she may be having twins because her doctor thought there may have been two heartbeats. She wants Brandon back together with her. He says no but knows he's going to have to spend time with her, especially since her pregnancy has been a difficult one. They eventually did find out that they're having a girl, which he is glad of, and he plans to go with her to her appointments because she's having trouble driving. Dear Lord, take care of the baby please, and watch out for her mom and dad.

Premonition- *the night before (Wednesday night) I dreamed about a serious storm. Patrice and I were going to get in line to buy tickets for something and were to meet Brandon and one of his friends there. They got there before us and were up front when we saw them. They did get our tickets and we all walked in the opposite direction of the line to go to some restaurant. The sky changed. It was around dusk but still very light then we all saw these huge charcoal gray, thick clouds literally rolling and moving very fast. Others were looking up, too. We got to the restaurant and there were people outside looking up and talking and inside at tables talking. It got dark inside suddenly- no lights, no candles. Then I saw a light switch and turned it on. The lights came on, not really bright but restaurant-dim. People looked as if nothing had happened. I saw Patrice smiling hard, talking across a table to someone. That's the last thing I remember before the alarm clock went off.* I don't know where Brandon was. Sounds like a vision but I don't know... I can't read too deeply.

March 17, later that day

I went to see my therapist today and I told her about my dreams and about Lana having academic trouble. The dreams are so detailed and are kind of long. Having therapy helps me to understand my troubles, but also makes me wonder if there's something else going on with me. She suggested a psychic for dream interpretation. Also, she's checking into the EMDR eye movement process to help with trauma and anxiety.

When I got to Miss Francine's (Lana's babysitter) house, she was mad or something and she felt offended or hurt because she thought I should have asked her to keep Lana late as a favor on Wednesday. I guess she thought my getting my hair done was something I expected to delay. It did, but the traffic delayed me even more. I ended up still paying her an extra fee so it wouldn't have been a favor. I don't like her much these days. I'll be letting her go after the school session ends.

Tomorrow is Reclamation and Rededication for Zeta Phi Beta and I also have a high school step show to judge. I've been watching step shows and I want to get a few practices in soon. I think Brandon is going to come by afterward. He is sounding a little more excited about his baby. I hope all turns out OK.

Does a house or place you frequented at some point in your life often appear in your dreams? Is that place just as it was in your past or is it different?

_____

_____

_____

_____

_____

_____

_____

_____

_____

_____

_____

_____

_____

_____

_____

_____

_____

_____

_____

_____

_____

_____

_____

_____

_____

Are You Guys Ready

March 20

This morning I saw Dad in my dream. It must have been after 4 a.m., because I woke up and checked the clock and closed my eyes again. *In the dream, I saw Daddy coming up the stairs- I think it was at the Kenmore house. It didn't look like this house completely- same layout though. He got to the hallway and asked, "Are you guys ready?" He had on a black suit, a white shirt, and something green. I'm not sure if it was a tie or something in his hand. His hair was dark- black or dark brown, mostly, with a little gray. Mom was coming up the stairs and I saw Daddy turn to head back down and he disappeared. I asked her if she saw him and she asked, "Who?" I told her Daddy just asked if we were ready. She didn't see him.*

Then we started looking for something- jewelry- for Mom. At this point, we were in her Florida house.

This weekend was decent. I had a good Saturday at the meeting and rededication ceremony. And I judged, with 7 others, a step competition at St. Francis Academy. That was actually pretty decent and fun. Brandon came over afterward and we had a nice night and morning. Good conversation as usual. We went to lunch around 12 and he headed home a little later. Gotta go to work…

Oh yeah, Lana had a good weekend with Ms. Cassia – they went to the circus and on Sunday after church, they went to a birthday party for Trey's daughter. She was wiped out and sleepy-silly when I got her last night. I love to see her so excited.

Walking Dream

March 23

I'm running behind so I've got to type quickly. *I did dream a walking dream last night. I was on my way home, I guess, and I had some kind of big bag on my shoulder or a backpack and it was late and dark. I was alone and was walking in alleys and through yards. I went through a yard and I saw two guys behind me on bicycles. One asked me to leave the gate open. I saw them again later and asked them where someplace was and if they had been there before. It made me feel a little better talking to them instead of wondering if they were following me. They went in a different direction shortly after. I went up some steps at one point. I saw streetlights and a lot of trees hanging that made the light dim or seem to flicker. For some reason, I had to turn around and go back where I came from, and I went the same path I started out on. On the way down the steps, I saw something running past me as if it was going into a yard or basement. There was a house adjacent with the same kind of steps leading into a basement opening. The steps were wooden and damaged. It was a dog that passed me. It started barking and growling and once I could see it clearly, it was moving closer. I remember lifting my foot to kick it but I don't think I connected. That's when I woke up.* Oh yeah, I was supposed to be in California. And, no, I wouldn't kick a dog- unless it was actually attacking. While I was procrastinating on getting out of bed, I recalled other walking dreams. *In one, I was in some downtown Baltimore area, and in another, I was walking in the 1400 block of Kenmore.*

The night before, I dreamed something that included taking pictures with both of my cameras and a governor.

The night before that, I had a blue & white dream.

Outside of all that, I am setting some dates to finish my project. The surveys for my Master's thesis are out there and I will be sending something to Dr. Jean-Baptiste to get it all approved. Also, I realized that I <u>am</u> going to do this- finish this degree. Somehow, I forgot and let myself get worried. Gotta go get a shower and be dressed in five.

Yes, Lord and Yes, Daddy- I'm trying to make good choices.

I can recall another of my single-digit years' dreams. This is one that, much like the floor of worms, makes me nervous just at the thought of it happening in real life. *In this dream, I was with a small group of about four people. I'm not sure if we were camp friends or neighborhood kids, but we were all about eight or nine years old. We were walking along a trail, one behind the other, talking and laughing. We came to a wooden bridge that appeared to be old and weak in places. The overall appearance was that it may have been sturdy, but time and weather had taken their toll. One of the group members stepped out hesitantly and slowly made his way across the bridge, which may have been about 20' across. Below the bridge was a creek with dirty water and tall grass along the edges and through the water. The others followed, one at a time. I was in the back of the group, bringing up the rear. I tip-toed across the creaking wood, trying to step where the previous kid had stepped, all the while, looking down at the water below. The bridge could have been 20' above the water or 5' above it. It wouldn't have made a difference to me. I was fearful but didn't want to get left behind, so I stayed with my group.*

Once we were all on the other side, we picked up on our jovial mood. We climbed rocks and shuffled our feet through the reddish-brown clay and dirt, making miniature dust clouds. After a while, we came upon another bridge. This one was made of dirt and rock and had an incline, arching over the water below. The creek below this one was very similar in width and appearance, but the dirt worried me a lot more than that wood had.

One by one, but closer together, we got on our hands and knees to climb and cross the dirt bridge. This one seemed longer since we were crawling. The dirt crumbled at the sides where it must have been really dry, flaking off with the pressure from the tips of our sneakers and fingers. The dust was in my face and I slipped, losing my balance a couple of times. I gripped the ground as if hugging my dearest elder. I kept my eyes open wide as I watched my friends getting further ahead of me, with the first one making it to the other side. A side-glance caught a glimpse of larger chunks of dirt and rock falling away into the water behind and below me. Hear me Lord, as I pray to get to the other side. He heard me, because as I opened my eyes after this brief prayer, I found myself on the safe side, still on my hands and knees but facing the direction from which I had come. The dirt bridge was still there, with pieces crumbling off and my friends were helping me up.

I have never cared for bridges, but bridges over water especially trouble me.

Daddy's Back

March 28, 5:45 a.m.

I dreamed about daddy last night. He was sitting in a chair or on a stool beside a table or breakfast counter talking with mom. Mom was in the kitchen on the other side of the counter. I came in and he said, "Hey, baby," and I hugged him. He said that he was back followed by something cliché or philosophical and added, "like Richard Pryor said," to it. (I don't remember it now.) We were all smiles and laughing. His hair was growing back, and his scar was visible. Mom was saying that he should stay in for a while before we let others know he is back since we don't know for how long. I asked about his sister, Aunt Estelle, and his brothers, and he said we'll have to think about just how to tell them.

During the stroke Dad experienced, there was bleeding on his brain. The doctors performed surgery on his head to relieve the bleeding and pressure, creating a scar.

I took off today to go to Lana's IEP (individualized education plan) meeting. Lord, help us keep Lana on track and to be progressive with her learning. My body is sore, my shoulders mainly. I don't know if it's my sleeping positions or what.

Detective in Boots and Olive's House

March 31, 5:28 am

Dear Dream Maker,

Why am I the special person who gets to see and feel in Technicolor while I attempt to sleep? I try to actually sleep and these thoughts and scenes come on like a television show.

On Wednesday night, I dreamed that I was a homicide detective and was working with two male detectives. We went to someone's house to wait on a warrant to acquire some information about the case we were working on. While we were there, we all got comfortable and I took off my boots- the black calf boots. I didn't mention my feet hurting or anything- I guess I just wanted to get them off. After some talking and whatever else we did, someone called or came in and told us that we got what we were waiting for and needed to go. I went to put my boots on and couldn't find them. I was rushing and said I had some tennis shoes in the car but knew they wouldn't look right with whatever I had on- something dark. I finally remembered where I left my boots, put them on, and went with the fellas.

No clue what all that means but Cathy, my counselor, thinks the shoes symbolize being grounded or who I am, depending on the style of shoe. I think they might represent some jobs I do.

Last night I dreamed that I was selling something like candles or bath products from a catalog and I went to pick them up from Olive's house. A couple of other people were there- not sure who they were. Her house was decent and in Dundalk or an area that looked like it and she said she really loved her home. She showed us around a little. I would have to draw it. It was cream-colored and carpeted in the front rooms and light shades in the dining room and kitchen, but I don't recall much else except there being a patio door that I could see from and it was nice outside- clear sky and sunny.

Keywords: detective, homicide, warrant, boots, misplaced, fashion conscious; sell, Olive (from college), house, tour, cream colored, carpeted, clear sky

Slow Fulla

April 4, 5:50 am

No, I don't have much time, but I have to put them down. *Sunday night I dreamed something about going through a big box or big selection of shoes. They weren't shoes I already have so that's the only way I realized that it was a dream.*

Last night, I was very restless. *I dreamed that I went to a wedding. I was dressed in a platinum colored pants suit and looked good. It was a white family's wedding. During one part of the dream, I was walking across a street with a group maybe going from the ceremony to the reception. The Carpers were there and Fulla was there but I didn't sit with them. Someone came into a room where I was with a bunch of people sitting down on the floor (all of us) for some reason, came to me and said, "The theme was cream and gold." I was supposed to wear one of those colors. Most were wearing some cream/ivory shades. I said that this was what I had and then said, "You're not in either color either," and she got a little flustered and walked away. I think she was the mother of the bride. Later on when people were leaving, and walking towards cars, I saw Fulla. He had a bandage around his head, and he was retarded (politically incorrect- but he was behaving is a slow way). I think he was standing and rocking, looking up and around in amazement, and I went toward him but not very close. I asked him if he had a ride. He nodded and I saw the Carpers a little ways off and they acknowledged that they were with him. I said good-bye and he continued smiling and rocking.*

I couldn't get back to sleep very well. This was around 3 am. Lana has a cold and was snoring heavily. Plus, my body is still very sore. So, I just thought about my friend Brandon and I fell asleep sometime later. It's time to get myself together. There's a field trip today to the community college. I hope all goes well.

Lord, I miss my Daddy and my old Fulla. I hope they're watching over us and smiling with you. Thank you and I pray that I am doing right with this big gift you gave me in Lana. I love her so much.

6:01 am

Background: The colors for our wedding were cream and gold.

Keywords: wedding, platinum, Carpers, Fulla, Me, sitting on the floor, wrong color, bandaged head, brain damaged, smiling rocking.

Turned into a Movie Night

April 12, Wednesday, 8:15 a.m.
I'm behind on writing but I do need to get these thoughts and dreams down.

Last night first:

I dreamed about Brandon and I walking somewhere like a park with two children. I don't know if they were ours together or his and mine. There was some other scenario before I dreamed another dream. I kept waking up because the TV was on and very bright and I thought it was the sun. We've been at mom's house in Florida since Sunday and staying until tomorrow evening. A short trip, but it's been good- flea market on Monday, Disney's Animal Kingdom yesterday, and today I will get some thesis work done.

The other dream went strangely- Brandon had come over to spend the night. It was a basement or lower-level room in a large house. We were talking when I heard people come in and I went into the big screen TV room. Dad was sitting on the couch and my cousin Jeannette was coming down the steps. Someone (her daughter, Monique, maybe) was with her. Jeannette said something about being tired and she went to the back bedroom and got in bed. I remember thinking- there goes our intimate night.

In the TV room, Dad was talking to someone- Carla Jackson (a teenaged student of mine). She had three children with her- one was 14. I asked if that child was hers- she said yes, and I asked how. She had to have been three or four years older than her. She said that she was molested and raped by her father as a young child and somehow got pregnant and the baby was now 14. Crazy huh?

Dad and Brandon met and talked some and it turned into a group movie/popcorn night. I don't remember actually hearing Daddy's voice, but I know he was talking.

I miss Dad a lot. I'm going to go by the cemetery today to say a prayer. Yesterday, I thought about when he took Lana and me to the park in Orlando. They rode the long slide and the go-karts there. He took us to Dinosaur World on the road leading to Tampa, too. Those were nice days. *I wish you were still here.*

When Lana and I left out yesterday, we passed the cemetery and I told her that I missed my daddy. She said, "I miss my daddy, too, but they will always be in our hearts."

She's great. Such a stuffy nose. I just love her.

The Long and the Short of it

April 16, Easter Sunday, 12 p.m.

Last night, Patrice, Lana, and I went to Fells Point and the Power Plant, after driving out to Harford County and having dinner. We met a few bikers- Sigmas. Cool people but Patrice attracted a dude with married man-in-denial syndrome. Anyway, I hope she finds whatever is best for her.

I dreamed that I dressed for school/work and I wore some kind of long shirt or shirt dress. By the time I got to school, I found it to be too short. I was running late and kept pulling on it. By the time I got to the class, I saw Erica Allen, the department chair, taking my students around the corner to another classroom. I had a drill sheet ready, but I just wasn't in the proper dress. The shirt kept rising.

Brandon's baby is expected to come on Wednesday. I guess she must be having the labor induced or a C-section. I miss him and wanna cry, but for what? The next few months may be hard on me regarding us. Let the little one be healthy, Lord.

Accident Scene and Copier Issues

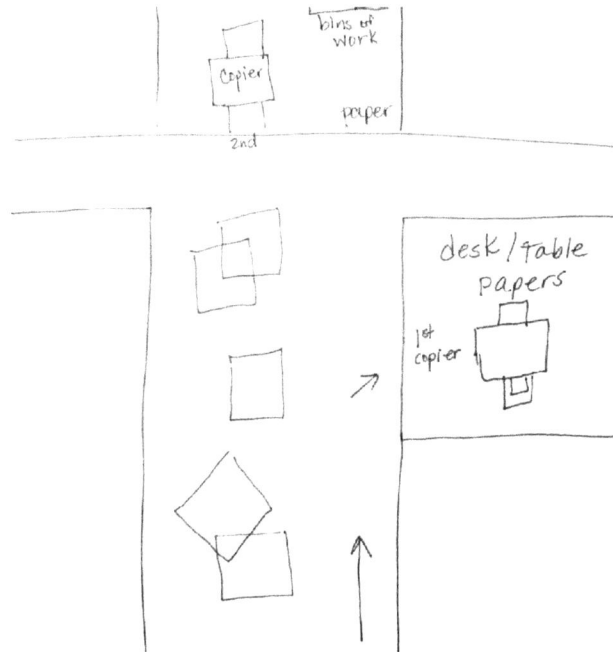

April 17, 10:00 a.m.

I tried typing this but as I was saving, I'm getting an extremely slow response with my computer.

Dear Dream Maker,

I had two dreams or partial dreams this morning. I fell asleep on Zorro last night after a long evening. Easter dinner and a reunion meeting were held at adopted cousins, Deana and

Emmanuel's home. The food was pretty good, and the kids enjoyed the egg hunt in their backyard. It was tiring just watching them, and Lana got the most eggs. Yay for her. After dinner, we met Patrice at our house and then rode over to Arundel Mills Mall to meet other family, Shelby and Joe. I had a couple of bags of clothes that they might be able to use for their daughter Harmony. They are a cool couple- have their ups and downs like everyone else but still stay together. We talked out there for almost an hour. Before they got there, we sat and watched a group of bikers' chit-chat and mount up to ride off. A few of them were nice looking and of course, the whole motorcyclist picture had great sex appeal. I would much rather see my friend Brandon on his motorcycle than be looking at some other guys, but they all have that appeal and I'll take what I can get.

The dreams: *in the first one I was driving my truck with Brandon, and we rode on some highway with sharp curves downhill. There were accidents happening further ahead of us but there wasn't any traffic buildup. There weren't many other vehicles on the road in either direction. As we came around one curve, I slowed down and saw a large, brown spot in one lane and a girl on something (maybe a motorcycle) turned over. She was white and her right cheek was against the ground. I got my vehicle around her OK and we must have pulled over because, in seconds, I was really close to her talking and asking her something. She did respond and I think Brandon was in the truck calling 911 for her. No other cars came by.*

In the second dream, I remember packing up things in a room. It may have been my classroom, but it wasn't the actual one. Somewhere along this, I went into a hallway and saw my friend Elayne. We talked and she needed to copy something, and I did too, so we started to walk. We saw a mother and daughter walk by- the mother was holding her daughter's hair- really long and braided, I think. The daughter had long hair past her feet and she was an older teen or in her early 20s. They had boxes in their arms. When we got near the copier, boxes were in the narrow hallway making it difficult to get through, so I moved what I could against the wall. At the one copier, someone left paper that was mixed blue and white with numbers at the bottom, and on page 100, the number was bold and large in the center of the page. At another copier, the same pile of mixed paper with numbers was in the go-through part of the printer. We used some of it but had to reprint when we missed the page that had the bold numbers on it. Must play 100 and 400 in the lottery.

I must get some housework done today. Back to work tomorrow.

Family Photos

April 19, 5:45 a.m.

Actually, it's 10:00 p.m. and I'm rewriting what I typed this morning because my Word program froze.

Always with the computer problems. There's a tear moving down my right cheek. I think I'm just tired. I went to bed late after getting the flight stuff together, watching TV for a while, and eating a very late dessert.

The dream was a split screen, I think. I was at a flea market somewhere and I don't remember much about that except for the scenery and walking around. And in the other part of it, I was looking at someone's photo album. It was Aunt Angie, on recollection. First, I saw a large, poster-sized picture of Uncle Charles or Uncle Derrick with granddaddy beside him. They looked a lot alike, but it was an old picture. Uncle Charles was on the left, as you look at the picture. Redd Foxx was a little to the right of Granddaddy and a step behind them in the background. It was a hologram, and it was taken at a flea market. The background of the picture was a moving crowd outdoors- not a big crowd, just a group of people looking at different things. The next picture was of Uncle Ashton laying on his stomach dressed in red with a few pieces of blue. He was maybe six- or seven-years old. He had his face in his hands and his elbows on the floor and his knees down and feet up and crossed. Big smile. I looked beside that picture and saw one of a young Aunt Nina in the same position facing the same direction to the left, looking at the picture, also wearing a red outfit with pieces of blue near the trim. It was almost like cowboy and cowgirl outfits. Kind of frilly.

I think this is when the alarm clock went off.

Yesterday, at Milford, I bumped into Roman for the first time in almost a year. I can see the appeal, but I was completely uninterested. I have no use for him.

A lot to rewrite but…

Brandon saw his daughter today. She was born this morning by C-section delivery. She was six pounds and two oz., healthy. He said he cried when he heard her crying. I'm glad he called. I really didn't expect to hear from him today, at least not this soon, plus he has family there- his mother and others. I think I'll send a card or a gift basket to him. I don't have much money in the bank with all these flights to pay for.

May 10th- in retrospect- I remember a vision of a baby to be born on April 19th. I told Lurena that it was hers. Hmm

Not my Student and Some Day-Dreaming...

April 26

Dear Dream Maker,

Last night I dreamed that I was asked to come to some room in the school to meet a parent about a notice they received for a book that had not been returned. They wanted to return the book, but also wanted to speak to me about the note. The student's face looked familiar but I wasn't positive about having been his teacher. Then the parent mentioned something about having Biology five years ago, and I told him I wasn't teaching five years ago, and that this was my fourth year at Randallstown. He acted as if he didn't believe me. He then pulled out the textbook and it was something really old that I never gave my students which confirmed for me that I wasn't his teacher. I'm sure there were other ways to figure out who taught him, but someone sent this father to argue with me. Crazy.

Keywords: school, book not returned, five years before, argumentative father, note- former crime scene coworker Omar Scott popped up in my dreams somewhere, too.

I am making progress on my thesis project- just a few more things to do and it will be over soon. Yesterday, all money necessary was given to the lawyer for Fulla's son. I guess it's his child. I hope they use it wisely because there is no more. I have only to pay my lawyer and close the account. I think I'll have to send them a copy of the closed account statement to further finalize everything. I had a moment where I was thinking of contacting the girlfriend to arrange for Lana and the little boy, Donis to meet. I will think about it more and maybe sometime during the summer. If things go as currently planned, we will not be living here for much longer, so I have to at least let Lana know about her half-brother. Some prayer will definitely be required here.

I went to Milford last night after having my dress for Ava's wedding fitted. I think I will just go there on Tuesdays and to Woodlawn on Thursdays, for now. I saw Roman in the parking lot. He reached out for a hug and stuck his tongue in my ear. Truly gross- I guess it only feels stimulating when I like the one doing it, so I am positive that there is no feeling left. He's got a lot of confidence though but not what I want or need now. I like my Brandon and know he likes me. It's a good feeling right now. Soon we are going to have to talk about any future between us as friends or if he thinks we can maintain any long-distance communication when I move. As a tear rolls down my right cheek this morning, I feel that I already know what will happen. We will call regularly for a while then things will change- issues with our children, meeting other people, and who knows. We might get a visit or two in before we realize that we love each other and can bring it together or we love each other and cannot bring it together so we'll have to let go. The reality is that it takes more than love to make a relationship work. Question is –do we have or will we have the other necessary components? Right now, we only have a true friendship and desire, along with some admiration, and fun. That's cool for now, because of our individual stresses. I'm just not sure what to hope for later.

Ordering Robes and a Song in Paradise

May 1

Dear Dream Maker,

Where do these dreams come from? *A few nights ago, I dreamt about being in some room like an office of a church and I was ordering choir robes. There were a handful of people there- male and female choir members who helped me to translate some of the design information I was to check off on the order form. The copy of the form had been copied so much or may have been a fax and was difficult to read. The robe they had was not very nice looking to me- a washed out burgundy with another shade of washed out pink- almost that mauve color like my carpet and there was a part on the front that had a shoelace kind of tie-up thing. They wanted more of the same- I disagreed but it wasn't my decision.*

Strange one.

This morning, after waking up around 3 something when Lana came in, *I dreamt about being either on some island or in another country and I went to visit a small community. I entered a house or large hut and there were two women at first. One woman was dark and didn't say much at all, just showed us around. I don't know who "us" was, but I know I was not alone there. The other woman was very pretty and really light skinned, nearly white. Her blonde/light brown hair had a weave pattern like a basket and was really different. She wore a white dress tied around her body with some jewelry at her neck, some bracelets and earrings. She was singing to herself, but loud enough that we could hear and her voice was beautiful. She sang and spoke in another language. I went over to her to ask if she understood English and she just smiled and put her head down. She was doing something with her hands and a pot- like preparing food or making something – not sure what. She went to a door and I saw papers in a pocket on the door. The top sheet had Archibald Anye on the top and she saw that I recognized the name and she said something to me including his name. We went outside the hut and she sang some more and did her craft while we sat in front of her on the ground. I stared at her hair and listened to her song mesmerized.*

This weekend was a downer. I spent a few hours on Sunday working on my thesis project, but most of Saturday, I spent inside with Lana who was a little on the sick side- allergies have a hold on us and I haven't found a medicine for her that works effectively. I wanted to get out yesterday, but knew I needed to get computer time in. I need to work on a sitter for my girl for the next few weekends. I thought about my dad a lot and about Fulla. Even got mad at him a few days ago for being such a jerk while we were together. It's strange how now I do a few of those things he wanted me to do- I think it was in the delivery and demand that made me not want to keep responding to him. The monies have been delivered to the Ortega family for the little boy, Donis. I was thinking about contacting her (the girlfriend) sometime this summer. I'll have to pray on that one. Really.

Brandon checks on me- thank goodness. He's putting in time with his daughter, which is good. His voice changes a little when he talks about her- kind of softens, like he's smiling. Nice. We need to talk soon- and go out on a real date. I miss that part of our beginning.

Keywords: church robes, poor quality form, burgundy, pink, tie; island hut, women, light-skinned, hair, weave pattern, blonde/light brown, white dress, jewelry, singing, other language, pot, papers, Archibald Anye

Have you ever created something in a dream (a design, a drawing, a song, etc.)?
Did you follow through and make that dream into something tangible?

_____

_____

_____

_____

_____

_____

_____

_____

_____

_____

_____

_____

_____

_____

_____

_____

_____

_____

_____

_____

_____

_____

_____

_____

_____

_____

_____

_____

Vision of a Burglary

May 4

Dear Dream Maker,

I almost forgot my dream- I remembered when I first got up, but I had to send a note to my former coworkers, Leona and Jonathan, and the dream temporarily slipped away. I do recall most of it now though.

For some reason I woke up at 1:04 a.m., then at 1:44- maybe Lana moved or something, then at 4:06 am. What's with the fours? Anyway, I got out of bed at 5:08 before the alarm for a change and came in here to get a little done. I know I need to start getting up a little earlier to go back to doing morning exercises or just for writing, but sometimes the bed feels pretty good or maybe I need to try to get to bed earlier. These last few nights have been long ones. Monday, I dropped Lana off after piano to get her hair done and we didn't get to sleep until after 11:30 p.m. and Tuesday night we went to the Teachers TABCO dinner. I thought I was getting an award, but that didn't happen. The people on the board had not received anything for me from Randallstown, so no award. Disappointed but not stressed about it.

Last night I talked with Brandon- he's feeling the drama with the baby's mother. I guess she must have something going on and he hadn't seen her and the baby in a couple of days- really stressing him. I listen and I can't truly advise but I will offer my opinion sometimes when asked. I'd rather him be attentive to his daughter and take the time and effort than not. I do miss him but I really need to put in time for the rest of my degree project. I sent out my SOS to Leona and Jonathan, my forensic/academic friends, for help in the final process. Hopefully, one of them will be able to help. It dawned on me the other day why I was so depressed over the weekend and miserable- that damn PMS. I really forget about it until after it hits me.

The dream- I was in a truck with my man- I don't know who he was, but he was tall- maybe 6'1" or 6'2" and on the lighter side, average build, and good looking. We put some tent-like thing into his SUV to take to his mother's for a cookout or party for the neighborhood children. When we got there, we had trouble getting it out of the truck. We were in Waldorf in an area I hadn't seen before. At his mom's, there were a couple of dogs and I remember thinking that it would be hard to get Lana around here with the dogs loose. After we got the tent thing in the yard, he took me to another place to see some of his friends. Dean

Brooks, from RHS, was there and we hugged. Dean went back to his house- very large. He had four dogs himself- a Saint Bernard, and three smaller ones that looked mixed. He checked on them toward the rear of the house, while I came inside.

There was some scene at this point where there was a staged burglary- he (the owner/perpetrator) used a bat to break a glass curio door and items were removed. He set the house alarm and opened the door, triggering the alarm. I think it was a demonstration of something or maybe a premonition within the dream because then, in a blink, everything was the same as it was before the curio case was broken. I remember the man's face, but I don't know him- maybe it's someone I have seen somewhere before. I can't think of an actor by name to fit the description, and I wish my drawing skills were better. I'll try to find a picture.

Got to get ready for work.

Monumental Cups

May 8

Dear Dream Maker,

Kama, my long-time girlfriend, showed up in my dream last night. In between naps, I dreamed about being high up in the cup of a huge building. It looked like a city hall and when I was trying to remember the dream as I got up, I saw former crime scene coworker, Omar Scott wearing something green coming out of a front door. He was smiling and talking to someone behind him, as if they were leaving work. The building had a dome and stairs on both sides and at the tops of the stairs were look-out cups. The cups were pretty big and when I made it up to one, I was telling Kama, who was walking with me, that I came up here before with some guy. Once I was inside the cup, I touched a side wall of it and the stone fell outward and into the water below. I looked over the edge hesitantly and saw the water and immediately, moved back. I think I said that it was time to go shortly after.

I woke up at 12 a.m. something, then 3:57, then 4 something. I feel rough- my throat is scratchy. I was a little emotional this weekend. Ava's wedding shower went okay- I wish we had organized some more games to make it even more memorable, but she did get some nice gifts. Dr. Ruby Smith, a dear lady, just popped into my head- I think she was part of another dream. I was speaking to her recently about something.

Well, once I left Soror Ren's house, I was supposed to be heading home to do some work but I decided to stop by Sheers to get my hair trimmed down. Ms. Connie did it this time and she was so nice. I did feel a little better when I left but it didn't take long before my spirits dropped again. I talked with Brandon for a little while between the wedding shower and the hair-do. He and I are both pretty down these days. He thinks that he isn't doing anything to help me and there really isn't much I could ask of him because listening to me is the most anyone can do. I just have to work the blues out myself. I do miss him though. My cousin Dana from Philly had called to try to get me out to Club CO-2 with her but I would have had to drive by myself, and my truck is having problems, plus I hadn't done enough of my homework. Lana went to stay with the Carpers for the weekend. I don't really feel like bashing them right now but they are pretty inconsistent. I'm glad I got over there so Mr. Carper could see that she needs his attention more often. She had her bike and she needs to ride more to feel secure on it. I just cannot do it right now. We'll see how it goes- if they want to get with her for a day or weekend.

I did get a chance to speak with Leona about my project and she was very helpful. She is willing to participate on my committee to get this thing finished. I will have to put in a few nights this week to get more done by the end of the month. Friday, I am scheduled for the LASIK eye surgery. I pray all goes well.

Diary Entry

May 10, 4:27 am

I have been up and on the computer since about 3:15 a.m., maybe. I don't know what made me restless last night. I thought I would spend a little time here to think about my thesis. I have to change a few things and will work some more on it over the weekend. I have to scrap the surveys- not as big a deal as it would have been a week ago. I do still feel somewhat depressed but it's lightening up. I will be finished by the end of the month. I talked with Leona for a while over the weekend. She's a great friend- always there for me and I love her.

My truck has been at the service center since Monday and I have a rental vehicle- a Nissan Armada. It's nice but it has as many glitches as the Dodge. I hope to be able to find another vehicle in the very near future- something smaller to buffer this gas issue, especially over the summer. Lana likes all the compartments and the spacious back seats. It is pretty cool to ride in something else but that coolness will wear off as soon as I pay the $600 to fix my truck. I'm considering trading it in, but I'll have to think about that a little later.

I looked back at my journal this morning and see that I have more and more typed notes. I know I type faster than I write on paper so that's cool. Only thing is the computer has headaches sometimes, making saving or printing a problem. I hope to be able to work on this repair this summer, too, among a bunch of other stuff. I was able to have someone work on the porch for me. Tobias (Vincent's dad) came over last Sunday. We (he) talked for about 4 hours out front. He's pretty cool- has a cool Jamaican accent. Not bad on the eyes, around 40-something, maybe 6', decent build, lots of philosophies on life and the state of the world. He took care of the porch for me yesterday and will be back maybe Thursday to re-check it and work on my banister. I'm glad I called. That's one less thing to take care for the house itself. I think the windows in Lana's room were the only other thing to get fixed. I'm going to plan for that in the fall. Maybe Tobias knows how to do it or can refer me to someone. He did mention knowing someone who teaches for motorcycle licensing. I can only check into it and see how it goes.

Tonight Lana has tutoring and tomorrow I will spend more time on editing my thesis. I think it will be fine. I pray that it will be fine. I haven't been faithful to church going at all this year. I just haven't thought hard about where I want to go to find comfort. I still like Israel Baptist Church but something has diminished in how I felt before.

I am missing my Brandon a lot- talking on the phone is cool but I would like to see him soon.

I'm thinking of having a graduation party on the Friday after we get back from California- the 23rd of June, since Mom will still be in town. I just have to decide if I'll do the restaurant thing or the house thing. I have to see how the money goes. I also have to decide about daycare for the summer and next school year for my baby. My neighbor Joyce said she'll have a spot but I need to check her rates and hours. I think I'm going to get dressed and lay down for a few minutes before I get moving full speed.

I am planning a breakfast for May 18th for my homeroom class- to hopefully buffer the anxiety I've been having as I remember Fulla. I told them about it and I hope they don't use the information insensitively.

Today is a good day.

May 18, 9:46 pm, Anniversary of that day

The day went OK. After first period, I had breakfast. I am tired- I've been awake since around 4:00 a.m. I baked a cake this morning before school. I fell apart after first period was over and went to Mr. Martin (Chemistry teacher) to hold me up for a few minutes. I did go to the cemetery after school and put a bouquet in the vase, cried for a little while, and headed to Walmart. I bought a few pieces of clothes for Lana and me and got the film I dropped off Monday. The first pack I opened had pictures of Dad with me and with Lana. I miss him so much. I miss Brandon, too. I'm lonely and I can't tell if Brandon really needs me anymore, but I know I need him. I sure could use his arms around me about now.

May 23, 9:07 p.m.

This afternoon after picking up my gown for Ava's wedding, Lana asked me, "What will happen to me if something happens to you? If you die, what will happen to me?" I told her that grandma would be here and would take care of her. She's so deep.

May 29, 8:16 a.m.

The wedding Friday was very nice- elegant. The hall, the decor, the service-all very sweet. The bridesmaids were beautiful, all of us. Only thing-during the reception, I got misty when they had their father-daughter dance. Ava's sister Anna walked me out and she and Sharon sat with me for a little while. Mr. Tyler was sweet, too.

I really miss my dad. I wanna talk to him and kiss his scruffy cheek. I wish I could talk with him about getting another car, about going to San Diego, about Brandon, about anything.

Lana spent Saturday night with Ms. Cassia and Sunday night with our neighbor's daughter, Brissa. I hope she had a good time. I have made some progress on my paper. I don't have much longer. I wish it would just be over.

Last night, I went to a movie with Brandon – one of the X-Men movies. It was OK but the storyline was disappointing. Clearly a lot on Brandon's mind and I've truly felt helpless and lonely right beside him. He didn't want any company, so we parked in the parking lot. I felt pretty bad, but I guess the problems between he and the baby's mother are really hurting him.

Uphill, Downhill, and B's Baby Girl

June 6

Dear Dream Maker,

It's already June and I haven't had quite as many dreams lately, but that's fine. I did dream about riding with my brother Davi about a week ago. I had spoken with him for a while and he talked about his marital issues and how heavy things have gotten for him. He's worn out financially and emotionally. I hope he decides what to do whether it be to work on their relationship or find a way to let it go soon. I hated the feeling of not wanting to go home to someone I loved but didn't like.

In the dream, we were in a car and he was driving. We had to go onto a bridge that was really steep. I don't know what city we were in but it didn't look like Lakeland or Baltimore. I started talking really fast and telling him that I didn't like bridges especially the ones over water and we just kept riding higher and higher. He told me to shut up, probably with a few curse words in between. I did and kept my eyes closed, too. We got to the peak and headed downhill and the ride down was like a roller coaster- fast and with that drop that makes the stomach weak and feel lost. It was short but detailed. I could see other cars and hear myself screaming and see my knuckles were tight and hurting from trying to hold on or keep myself from going too far forward by pressing my hands against the dash above the glove box. Crazy.

A couple of nights ago, I dreamt about Brandon. These are rare but I like to see him pop up sometimes. *We were laying in a bed- not mine or his, but a queen or king sized, and he had his baby girl with us. We were talking and playing with her and he was holding her up. She had just a T-shirt on and no pamper. I told him he was bold to let her hang that long with no diaper on and he sat up to get one and let me hold her and then she started peeing.* That was funny, but not funny. But that was the extent of it.

I am now 3/5th through with the thesis. I am working on the analysis today and hope to be done by Friday. I need to submit everything by Monday, my deadline. Everyone has been very helpful with me. I am excited about graduation and when I went to RHS' graduation at Towson last Saturday, I just felt the tears. I am very happy for the babies that came into RHS with me. I was also thinking about my graduation and the fact that my dad won't be there in person. I miss him so much. Yesterday morning was the first time since he died that I saw a CBT Transportation (the company he had driven for) truck on the road. I was on the way to work and saw it and the tears just came. I wanted to call Alex but don't have his extension handy. I will call soon.

I bought a new vehicle- a Chevy Equinox. It's nice so far- very different from the Durango. I hope the gas mileage is better than the Dodge. After school yesterday, I saw that my ex, Roman left his card and a request that I call him- "Please call me" and his numbers on my window. Not necessary. I really don't want to talk with him and he had my numbers- no need to call. I am a little curious though.

What to do....I am having a party for my graduation on June 23rd. I hope I can get everything together before we go away to San Diego. I am excited about the whole trip to California with my mom and Lana. It should be nice. Gotta get a little done- like write Fulla's brother Mark back- he's going through some mess with Tiffany and I pray he's alright.

Later.

Diary Entry

July 5, 10:45 p.m.

I am so very depressed right now. I went to take my motorcycle learner's permit test today and failed. I can get over that- I'll just have to review so more and go back early next week. I was at the MVA for about 90 minutes so I guess that's about average.

I was supposed to go visit Brandon this afternoon but something is wrong. That's part of why I've felt so shitty this evening. I woke up feeling washed out and just out of it- maybe because I haven't been eating right and I went to sleep around 3 a.m. The rain isn't helping at all. Lana is at Cousin Cyres & Noelle's until tomorrow. It's very quiet here and I miss my girl, but I think something is really wrong with Brandon and me. I need to talk with him and that was on my agenda for this afternoon until he called to tell me that he would be on-call because of the weather and if I call him and he doesn't answer to leave him a message. What kind of crap is that? He's been missing time with me more lately than ever and I understand about rain and having work to do when others are on vacation. No problem with that part- just not understanding the leave-a-message part. I always leave a message when he doesn't answer. Also, he has never gone to work and told me he would be unavailable. I don't want to over-analyze but it just falls in with what I need to hear from him: where is this thing going? I love him and feel like we could grow but we haven't put much effort into doing enough together stuff. I enjoy his company and the way I feel when we're together yet I think I want more and I really don't think he knows what he wants from me or us. He said the other morning that he needs to be more decisive about spending time with me. That could go both ways- more time or less. My first suspicion unfortunately is that he is spending time with the baby and her mother and is or has gotten intimately involved with her. That would go against much of what he has said about her but I really don't know. It's a feeling that something is not right.

I am lonely right now and miss my Brandon but we have become pretty stagnant and I don't really see a way up. I would love to plan a get-a-way for us or just go do something with his friends or mine. Movies, bowling, cards, midnight stroll, anything just to see his eyes and feel his arms around me. Yes, I would be disappointed if he told me that he was seeing someone else, but I would much rather hear it from him than wonder and have it confirmed some other way.

When we do talk soon, I need to ask-
Just how he feels about me,
If he has been out with anyone else,
If he sees me in his future,
What goals he has for himself,
What he is doing about his daughter and custody,
Has he considered that she may not be his at all,
How he expected our friendship to move or did he…

I remember thinking that when we first started to get to know each other, he said that he gets bored easily in relationships. I figured that this might last a couple of weeks or maybe a month but who knew? I've always felt that I have been pretty dull and uninteresting. What's the appeal from his perspective?

Also, I haven't heard from Dr. Stein on my thesis yet and the grading period is nearly over. I wrote to Dr. Jean-Baptiste this morning and he responded to say that Dr. Stein is fine and just to keep trying to contact him. I don't want graduation to have been in vain or even prolonged. I want my raise and my accolades so that I have whatever is needed to get applications started for my job search. I will be updating more on my resume this week and need to finish some reunion stuff as well. I will be glad when that is over and then the paramedical biology class starts. I will have to spend a little time on the computer getting to know some info for that subject soon. Mom wants us to come to Florida to visit before we get back to school. I don't really want to go but maybe I can set up an interview or two somewhere near Lakeland. I will consider Jacksonville, Orlando, Charlotte, Columbia, and some other unknown places. This is pretty big. I am very scared but I don't know what else to do- I don't want to stay here anymore. I miss my Dad and I'm getting tired of being lonely even when I have someone around. That's a crappy feeling, too.

I need to check into getting the internet switched to the desktop and getting this laptop repaired and cleaned or investing in a new one. But I need to get my bills in check a little better and get my eye surgery paid off first. Always working on something.

I think I had better go put my pajamas on and get a little TV time in or read a little. I'm getting tired and yet I don't want to sit in the quiet of my room and think about what I don't have next to me. What the hell do I really want from him? Honesty. I just have that nagging feeling that something is wrong.

I can't accuse, but I do have to get some of my questions answered. I miss him, but I can do without this funky feeling.

Please Lord let my uneasiness be settled and any missing information or lies be brought to the light. I pray there is no need for my confusion and doubt and that it is removed. Please take care of my Brandon and of me. Thank you for all you have given me and Lana and given me through Lana. She's the best. Help me to be more patient with her and teach her the importance of music and practice, persistence and diligence, ambition and motivation. I love her so much. I could be wrong about my lack of emotional peace but sometimes I am right on the money or could have just been a fool for a lot longer than I have realized. That would suck.

I need to get Lana's party planned.

Diary Entry

July 12

What a strange flow of days this week! On Monday, Lana and I fell apart. She started her summer bridge program. That evening she didn't have anyone available to play with so she started to cry. She must have been thinking about some things and she broke down to missing her daddy. She really wants a brother or sister and a father. I tried to console her and told her to cry as much as she wanted to cry. She let it out and then got to missing her granddad. That got me to the point of breaking down, too. We were a mess for a little while then I said for us to stop crying on the count of three like she does when she's trying to get off the phone with my mom. It didn't work right away, but she suggested we count to twenty. That helped and we called my mom and left a message. Mom called us back about a half hour later and she spoke with Lana. She told her to look up at the stars in the sky at night and see her dad or granddaddy and that they are always with us, watching over us. We were alright for a while but I had a hard time trying not to start bawling all over again.

We've been getting ready for the reunion and my laptop had an aneurysm. It will not open on the internet because of a mini PC card problem. I've been wanting to get it repaired and cleaned but now, I have a new one. I bought it yesterday at Office Depot. It's okay, but I'm not hyped up about it yet. I am such an impulsive buyer. I just got that bill down. Oh, well.

Today, I went to retake the learner's permit test. I didn't get it this time either. I have to wait at least a week to try again. I think I'll get it next time. I went to the cemetery afterward. Today would have been our 9th anniversary if we had stayed together. I bought flowers and stayed a few minutes. I do miss the knucklehead. Mostly for Lana.

When she was crying the other night, she asked me- why can't you find a husband? That's sucky but I told her that it isn't quite that easy. The man has to be good for both of us. She mentioned her attempts to get me a husband. Too funny, but scary at the same time.

Brandon is going through a lot of mess with his daughter's mother. One thing that is truly horrible is the fact that there are little girls like my baby who desperately want and need a father and then there are women like his other who are intentionally keeping the baby away from the father for their own selfish reasons. I guess I could understand better if he were abusive or had a screwed-up history, but none of that seems true. I feel for him, but at the same time, I really can't do much to help. I include him in my prayers. I miss him too, but I really feel helpless and left out at the same time. I already know that he doesn't want anything more from me but I don't really want to let him go. I have started looking into other jobs and a couple have potential. We'll see how it goes, but I think I'll have to lighten up on the gifts and contact- it's been minimal anyway, but I've grown attached and don't get the feeling that I need to be here in this emotional place too much longer. Just prolonging the hurt.

Got to get back to reunion stuff…We leave tomorrow for Norfolk.

Diary Entry

July 22, 10:52 p.m.

I haven't written in a little while, not because there was nothing to write, but because I just haven't sat still and focused on my thoughts enough to put them down. The reunion is over and it went very well. The slide shows and pictures went over great. I may be able to sell a few copies once I save them to disks. I'll have to work on that very soon. I miss my dad being there and being here to fuss with or just saying hello. Since I last wrote, I think, my wedding anniversary date passed. That was a rough day and the days before it. A few days before then, I had a really bad feeling about Brandon that I wrote about and it was semi-true- something bad had happened in reference to another female. The female turned out to be his daughter. He had been allowed time with her but then the mother, in her frustration with him, returned everything he had bought for the baby to his doorstep. He was truly hurt, and she threatened to disappear with no contact with him and his family. Crazy. I don't really understand her mentality, as it's been described to me, but I would hate to have to deal with an infant totally alone or at least without some prospect of help from family. I guess I did deal with that feeling with Lana, but family (outside of Fulla) was available if called upon. Anyway, it limits the time we have had together and I am so lonely for him. I just miss him. I love my sweetie but have not told him and mainly because I know his feelings are not the same and also because he has a huge stressor to deal with. His court dates are approaching and I wish him the best, but from my perspective, he's not as proactive as he could be for the baby's care. Maybe I just don't have all the information, which is very possible. We don't share enough. I get down about our relationship sometimes- we're friends first, but then I want more and I don't think he has room for more, especially right now.

DR. LEGGIE L. BOONE

Last Monday, I met my visiting brother Davi and his wife Sophia at Nick's house. Yes, Nick, my first crush, Davi's good friend growing up. He looks good, the same as he did 17 years ago. He remarried and they have 2 daughters. His wife wasn't very warm to me when I first got there, but she's okay- attractive and petite build. They have a nice place in the northeast area near the county line. Other neighborhood friends, Nigel Clark and his wife, were there also. Damon Townes stopped by and it was nice to see that they had kept in touch. Lana enjoyed the girls and is still asking to see them again. I couldn't go back there but I did send them an invitation to her birthday bowling party. Last Tuesday, I took Davi & Sophia around to visit a few people and the last stop was Mr. John and Mrs. Camilla Jenkins' house on Kenmore. They are funny and always have been very nice to us. It was good to see them again. They have been married almost 40 years and doing fairly well- a few health concerns, but holding on pretty good. Their son Robbie came in as we were about to go. He looks good- paid me the same compliment and was making a suggestive comment when his mother informed me to pay him no mind. He had been married and divorced 3 times and wasn't any good. Enough for me. Curtis Shepherd, from around the corner, was out front when we were heading to the car and recognized me. When he asked about Davi, I called him outside and they chatted for a while. Patrick B. showed up, but I was inside and didn't see him. Curt called Davi later to find out my status. I always had a thing for Nick, but never really paid Curt any mind. We spoke for a few and he gave me his number. I really am not interested but I bumped into him today at Rafferty Mills. I went there to get Lana's school uniforms and he saw me in the store. We talked some there and I gave him my numbers. I did end up calling him this evening. He's nice enough but still not interested. I guess my mind is stuck on Brandon. Yesterday, when I spoke with him (Brandon), I felt crappy and just told him that I was PMSing. I guess I was, because I feel better today. I felt so helpless for time and lonely- just miserable. He told that all he needs of me right now is for me to be understanding. I guess I can do that. It's hard to care for someone and not be able to really move forward with the feelings. Things happen for a reason. My head was so cloudy that I didn't recall even talking with him the day before nor him telling me that he was working overtime Friday. Crazy, again. To miss someone so much that I don't remember talking with them. I don't understand that myself.

Ava and I went to Artscape last night. We saw Adrian and Steve Roundhill. I still love my Adrian. Who knows? So fickle. If things don't work out with Brandon, maybe…Anyways, I fussed about his lack of returning my calls and what happened today- I called and he hasn't called back in over 6 hours. Oh well…

I'm still not completely finished with my thesis- I have to do a PowerPoint set-up (news to me) and wait for the approval forms to be signed so I can get the final document bound, and send it all to the department chair. I hope there are no more glitches or at least that the forms get signed very soon. I want my raise.

I have started job hunting and have only come across a few forensic positions. I will be contacting a couple of agencies when Lana and I go to Florida in a couple of weeks. I will check into the Department of Law Enforcement in Jacksonville and the West Palm Beach area. I talked to Cousin Naomi today in North Carolina. She mentioned Raleigh as a place I might consider. We promised to keep in touch.

I started the Paramed Biology workshop- it's pretty interesting. I think I might be able to get into it after all, but I still am opposed to learning/teaching a new subject when I know I am planning to leave RHS. I am so very scared about taking such a big step but I know I want to be a little closer to my mother and brother. Aunt Vinnie said she may be right behind me and that would be great too. She's the coolest aunt.

Cousin Benton went into the hospital this morning. He had a high fever and signs of pneumonia. The doctors feel he may have been exposed to tuberculosis. He is in my heart and prayers. Uncle Charles had a scare- a near collapse from heat exhaustion a couple of days ago. What's going on with the men in my family?

While we were in Norfolk, a song came on the radio that stuck in my head until I bought the CD. I found out that it was an Eric Benet tune and bought the 3 different ones that were in the music store. I finally played them on Wednesday and found out it is called- I Wanna Be Loved. I like it and it is fitting. "I'll let my heart take its chances just to be loved by you." I will put in a little more time on the piano and some drum time this week coming. I have no true excuse. I want to get the scrapbook mess off my table by mid-week and get my computer room in order. It's rough. Lana has a birthday party to go to tomorrow afternoon. I'm planning to go to the Copeland family church in the morning and Cousin Tammy is coming over to help take care of Lana while I go to the workshop. I bought her a small gift and hope all goes well this week.

Dear Lord, please take care of Uncle Charles and Cousin Benton. I love them both very much. Thank you for everything you have done for me. For my little princess and her crazy/beautiful friend Delorean, I thank you. For giving me the endurance and strength to handle my courses and complete my degree, I thank you. I ask for peace for my mother. I ask for guidance in my job search and relocation. I also ask for peace and strength and guidance for Brandon. I pray he knows that he means a lot to me and that our relationship is important. Help me to be strong in understanding his stress and to be a help to him as you see fit. I also pray for his baby girl, that she may not be hurt by the disruptive behaviors between her parents. I ask for emotional and mental peace for Aunt Regina also. Please take care of my family. I love them all. Thank you for the time we had together and for sending my brother this way for a while. He's crazy and I love him, too. Thank you for all that you have done for me and my family and friends. In Jesus' name, Amen.

Who has been a frequent player in your dreams? Your parents? Siblings? Cousins? Spouse? Friends? Coworkers? Are they as active in your reality as they are in your dreams?

_____
_____
_____
_____
_____
_____
_____
_____
_____
_____
_____
_____
_____
_____
_____
_____
_____
_____
_____
_____
_____
_____
_____
_____
_____

Vicious Cycle, Producer Candace, and Boat Truck

July 24, 10:36 a.m. (in Paramed. Biology at Sparrows Point)

Last night, I dreamed about Fulla- an argumentative abusive relationship. Once I realized what I had dreamed, I was very down. *Fulla and I were at some kind of garage or warehouse, and he went through the whole cycle of building me up to feel OK about making a decision or something to tearing me down and outlining why my choice was not the right one. I was really hating him for that- I could see the expression on his face. Disgust, distrust, and arrogance.*

Later on yesterday, I was checking the safe for a new checkbook and I felt our wedding rings. That was emotionally draining for a few minutes.

This morning I dreamed about Cousin Candace, her sister, Cousin Teresa, and I sitting in a booth talking somewhere. Candace told us about a film she produced. We were surprised and she went into some of the work she had put into the project.

That may have come from my conversation with Teresa at church Sunday.

My other dream was at first on the water- a pickup truck rack. The bed of the boat could fit a bunch of people. I was driving this thing. Brandon was in another boat trying to guide my parking.

I want to be Loved

July 28

Dear Dream Maker,

I don't have much time as usual, so…

Last night I went to bed at ~12:30 a.m. and woke around 5 something then at 6:36 on my clock. The clock has been set for 7:10 all week. Anyways, the dream was about this evening with Brandon. I spoke with him on the phone Thursday for a while and let him know in the most roundabout way that my feelings are pretty strong for him. I have a friend that is going through something…she feels something more for the guy she's been seeing than she thinks he feels for her…may be love…can't tell him because of the fear that the feeling isn't the same…

He asked if she were from out of state. No, very local. Didn't take much else to figure that I'm my own best friend.

The dream-*I dreamed about falling asleep at around 9 p.m. and missing out on spending time with Brandon. I woke up early and went to meet Cynthia somewhere. We were at a pavilion of some kind and were looking around trying to plan some event. Then we were in a hotel room. The phone rang and she answered. It was 9:00 a.m. and it was Brandon. She talked with him for a minute then put it on speaker. I got up and picked it up to speak directly and apologized for missing our date by oversleeping. Then somehow, I was with Cody, my singing partner from high school. We were walking and talking and she was singing. I started singing afterward. I did Eric Benet's "I Wanna be Loved" and she backed me up. I didn't sound very good in my dream, but she didn't care.*

Strange stuff.

Anyways, I've got to think about just what we need to talk about tonight regarding us. I do want to grow with him, but we don't spend enough time together for that, nor do I know if he wants to build something serious with me. I guess that would be important. I understand being considerate to his current issues- that's not really a problem for me, but I have kept my feelings to myself for a while, because of it. I know he has a lot on his mind and at the same time, so do I. I want to leave this place. I want to stay with him or find out if he can go with me. I've never forced my little girl on him because I didn't want her to grow attached and he be temporary. So many little things that add up.

Got to go....

Diary Entry

July 31

I started to write this morning but was able to find my teachers training group and went to UMBC to get information on their collegiate paramedical program. The speaker looked and sounded like the firearms examiner, Spence Rosen from the crime lab. I need to call him and Lt. Marshall. I plan to edit my thesis between tonight and tomorrow so I can get it in the mail by Wednesday. I got my new college ring in the mail on Friday- real cute.

My weekend was pretty bad. I was supposed to meet Brandon Friday, but I guess I must have really added that last straw for his nerves when I told him sort-of where my heart is. Anyway, he told me that it wasn't going to work. Of course, I asked what wasn't going to work. He said us. He tried to explain all that's been going on with him including additional drama with the baby's mother. Seems like she truly knows how to push his buttons and is really in control. Every weekend. On top of her, something is going on with his father, and he also has a major ticket to think about so he feels he can't give me what I deserve in a relationship. Am I hurt? Yes. I did tell him that I won't bother him but that I'm here if he needs to talk. He also mentioned suicide and I really didn't know how to handle that part of the conversation. I told him about my vision about that a couple of months ago. I did email him just to let him know that I care about him and know that he'll get through this somehow. When or how, I don't know but I will include him in prayer.

After talking briefly with him that night, I rode around for a while and ended up at the Harbor- got some ice cream and went to the Power Plant cut. I just didn't feel like going home. Lana had stayed over with Elayne. While down there, I saw L.J. from school with a group and called Patrice. I told her about the disintegration of Brandon and I and she kind of annoyed me by suggesting that I go to the gym with her to look at guys. Who wants to keep looking at something they can't have. I don't want to start some new crap anyway. Later on, I saw a couple of ThunderDogs (bikers) pull up with women on their bikes. Duane saw me but didn't speak. Don did come over to me and talked for a minute. He's sweet, I also saw Stanley Johnson, a student from school and someone else I can't remember right now. While I was at the fountain, milking my McDonald's lemonade, I saw a guy who looked like Brandon. Maybe my mind was just messing with me. I half-expected him to ride down there, but I don't know what I would have done if I had seen him. I headed home and went to bed after shedding my tears.

Saturday, Elayne brought Lana by with some peach cake to try to cheer me up. I love her. After she left we went to Aunt Vinnie's to drop off a gift for Cousin Mesa's baby shower. I really didn't want to be around too many people. We came home and I tried cleaning. I had already moved the couch and futon and just couldn't think of anything to do with myself. I tried sleeping but couldn't and later on Cousin Alissa and her boys came by for a visit. I wrote to Brandon that night just to let him know I felt horrible not talking with him but wouldn't be a bother. Later on, I saw that an old pen pal was online so we started a chat and I stayed on the computer with him for a few hours. He's funny and fresh, 40 and a Navy sergeant. He should be in from Japan in December for a short break, then return. Maybe we'll get together. Who knows.

Sunday, Lana and I went to Six Flags with Cousin Alissa and her boys, Kevin and Keith. She and her husband are going through some stuff. I hope it works out some kind of way. We had a decent time and the kids had a ball in the water park area. There were a few good-looking fathers out there with their kids. I saw one of my students there – Brandon Short. He's a nice kid. After we got home I remembered that I needed to get Cousin Tammy so she can get Lana back and forth to school. Got her and came home tired- Brandon called while we were getting our showers. Surprised, was I. (sound like Yoda) He just kind of thanked me for giving him space to get things straight. He said that he went to the beach and just walked to try to get his thoughts in order. He just wanted to let me know that he's okay. I'm glad he called but I won't call him yet. I don't want to press him for my company or anything, like I realized I had been doing. If or when he wants to see me or do something, he will have to make the plan. I'll just love him from a distance.

I also talked with Curt from the old neighborhood last night. I don't want to mislead him and have him thinking I really want to try to get anything started with him. Just not really interested.

I'm coming down with something- a cold or serious allergy issues.

I've been documenting my sleep for a few days. I'm going to make an appointment for the sleep study very soon. The dreams and visions plus the regular headaches are getting to me.

Bad Class and Shop & Slide

August 10

Last night, I dreamed that I had students come to my classroom for the first day of school. The room was really small and only about eight kids of the 20+ expected showed up. I started to go over my rules and syllabus with them. Some bad kids showed up and tried to disrupt class. For some reason, I was screaming at them. Screaming has never been my thing.

Some other dream led me to a mall. In one store, I was with two other people and saw Ms. Snow from RHS. She had blonde hair-natural, brushed out, long and pulled away from her face. Weird coming together. Ms. Combs, another RHS teacher, was also around, trying to get people to donate to something. I left the mall and came outdoors to a courtyard area- the stores faced the outside area. We were high up and I saw a huge slide like at a water park. I went to it, looked down, and saw the ocean. I got on the slide with my bags, slid fast and hit the water but came up quick and grabbed a huge square package (like a child's toy ½ house) and floated with it to a pier or walkway and climbed out.

Keywords: school, first day, disrupt, 8, 20; shopping, outdoor, high, slide, fast, ocean, float, Zara Snow, Combs

Hole Blue Waterfall

August 15

Dear Dream Maker,

At the Tampa airport. We're heading back home. I didn't go to the cemetery once this time. I wish I had. *Sunday or Saturday night, I dreamed about tripping into a hole. I was waist deep in this ditch and someone came to try to help me out. The guy helping pulled me out and fell into another hole, but it was much deeper. He needed much more help than just me, so I called others and ropes and pulleys were set up to get him out.*

I had other dreams, but don't remember them.

Last night, no Sunday night, I dreamed something about the book I had just finished reading (Out of the Blue). The dream had me in the water by a beach searching for something.

I just remembered another of Saturday night's dreams. *I was in a waterfall catching things that resembled big hair combs, just like Lana's computer game that I got stuck on.*

Last night, I dreamed something about a huge warehouse or storage space. I was getting things out to sell at a yard sale. There wasn't much left. Patrice was there and Elayne, with her boys. Then I was in Cousin Cyres' truck up front and some guy was in the back. We were going someplace to play cards. I don't remember much more.

Keywords: hole, help, man, ropes; book, water; storage space, yard sale, Patrice, Elayne, Cyres, play cards.

Lana and I went to Webster Flea Market yesterday. There were two stalls with puppies in cages. She liked them in cages and even petted them outside of the cage. She liked the Dachshund a lot and a Powder Puss (Shih tzu mix), the Schnauzer, and one of the Terrier (Yorkie, I think) mixes. I will look for a very small breed puppy starting this week.

Sick Cooper and the Two Terrances

August 16

Dear Dream Maker,

Last night, I dreamed about some people from school. One part had me in a storage room and someone had opened the door for students to come in. They wanted to buy things from the back instead of what was out in the front sales area. Raquel Cooper (former department chair) was back there and complaining because the room wasn't open to sales. Anyway, she helped a few kids out then told them to leave and closed up the room. Strange to see this petite, dark lady in a dream.

Then somehow we were in a car like a station wagon. Raquel, myself, Erica Allen (current department chair) and Raquel's husband. I had never met him but he was tall and looked like the guy who played Kendall Martin on the Cosby Show (Denise's Navy husband). We had ice all through the vehicle, which was melting, and it wasn't freezing us. Kendall guy was sick and puking into the ice and scooping up water with his hands to rinse his mouth. We all looked at him and Raquel said, "That was disgusting."

I was thinking- That's your husband. That ride lasted for a few minutes. Minimal conversation- I think we were going to a doctor or hospital. I don't know who was driving. The seats in the back were like in a limousine.

In another part, I was walking down a hallway (a school) with Terrance Diggs (student). He was telling me that he is in my paramedical biology class and that there is another Terrance in the class. I couldn't think of the boy's name and Terrance D said it was Justice. I just agreed and thought it must be that name.

I just remembered the other Terrence's name- Patton. Terrance Diggs was speaking with a lisp for some reason- or maybe he was stuffy with a cold. He didn't sound like himself.

House Hunt and Out-of-the-Way Ride

August 18, 6:56 p.m.

We return to school/work on Monday. I'm going in today to put some stuff in my classroom. Ready is never the right word for returning to work at the start of the school year.

First, last night's dream: Fulla and I left for work together, working for two different police agencies with some distance between locations. When we talked, I told him that it is time we started looking for a new house. We can look at some that he picked and some I picked to be fair, but we have to consider travel time to our current jobs. He was cordial in this one. Once I woke up and realized that he was in my dream, I thought back to my packing to move from Nachman Rd. and the whole physical separation, even down to sleeping in another room and him coming to sleep beside me.

Wednesday night's dream had me someplace with a girlfriend, maybe Patrice or Ava. We met a group of four guys, and they were nice and not bad looking. They said their names, but I can only recall that one started with A- something like Adrian (I miss him a little.) *They mentioned where they were going, and I needed a ride so I was invited to ride with them. Not too bad until they stopped in a row house neighborhood similar to Kenmore Road but with very few trees and no porch awnings. One guy needed to drop off a card to a friend or family member because of a death. We talked and when he got out, I looked around and saw Ms. Elizabeth (Lana's great-grandmother). I didn't want her to see me in a car with four guys, so at lowered down and tried to stay out of sight. She was carrying a dish with food, and someone met her at the steps to help her with it. I sat up to get out and the dream ended.*

August 19, 9:15 p.m.

The dreams. I need to catch up. *One I had Thursday, I think, had me with two guys (I don't know who) and we were setting up bombs/explosives between something that looked like mattresses. We separated and I went out toward the back way. I didn't get out fast enough and the bombs went off. I found a group of kids and tried to calm them and get them to a safer place. I left them and walked away down a long hallway. I saw a man at a counter, a vending counter, and asked him for directions someplace. He told me where to go and I left. I contacted Cousin Scarlet somehow and she told me to go to her house. I needed to change my shirt. I was wearing something white and sleeveless, and I didn't want anyone who may have been around earlier to be able to point me out by describing my clothes. I went to the house and saw clothes hanging on the clothesline with clothes pins. I got two T-shirts from the lines and changed into one and put the other in my purse or bag. I left there and that was it.*

Getting sleepy, but there is more. We're working on getting a dog. A dachshund, either a boy Dorkie or girl Doxie.

Has your dream ever made you call someone who appeared in it, just to check on them? Dreams have a way of bringing some of our deeply imbedded thoughts closer to the surface.

Bus Trip to Reception, Got Left, Game Room

September 6

Dear Dream Maker,

I've been slow on writing a few things down, but I had a long detailed one this morning. It's 5:40 am and I have already fed the puppies (we got a girl Dachshund and a boy Dorkie) and will have to get dressed very shortly. Anyways, *I was on a bus trip- to where, I don't know, but the bus was like a Greyhound, stopping at different rest places and stations. My mom, Aunt Angie, Auntie K, maybe Aunt Bridgette, and a few other familiar faces were there.*

We reached one stop and there was another bus there. We got out and went inside of a very nice hotel with a banquet area in the front portion. There was a small reception going on and when we got inside it turned out to be Cousin Wendell and his new wife's wedding reception. There was a table with large platters with huge pieces of meat on it. There was a big roast and a ham and stuff like that. There were other trays that had tiny serving dishes. We hugged and kissed everyone and talked with the new bride. She said that she had lost 130 pounds and now weighed 150, but somehow I recall the number 290. Not sure how that adds up but she seemed nice and Cousin Wendell looked healthy and happy. Someone looked out of the window and found that our driver was signaling us to come on and we helped a little with clean up (as we do) and had to say goodbye. I was the last helping with the tiny dishes that had melted butter in them. They were silver or some similar metal and had a small lid inside of each of the bowls. I went to leave and the bus was gone. I didn't have a phone to call my mother so I ended up staying with the new couple for a while. They showed me through the hotel. The last part I saw was a dim room with high ceilings. There were shelves like in a store stacked high with different types of games and there were stairs that led to a game room to play whatever people bought or rented. I picked up a bowling ball- not a true, heavy one but a regular sized one and dropped it. It rolled towards the open doors and kept rolling. I went to try to catch it and that's where it ended.

On reflection, maybe she said 140. I'm not sure.

I dreamed a few nights back that Brandon, who I haven't been talking with that much, told me that he met someone and that they had been intimate. Aloud, I wished him the best and hoped she made him happy, but inside I was torn up then I decided to tell him just what I felt and he got an earful of how I wanted more and yet he had time to go out with whoever he chose but couldn't make a plan to spend time with me and how much that told me about his true feelings. I understood his issues with the baby and was willing to still be a friend, but I guess I have realized that he isn't my friend or anything more. Sucks but that's reality. Not exactly a dream.

Gotta go get ready for work.

Barbershop Walk

September 8

Dear Dream Maker,

Yesterday evening was very surprising. Lana was afraid of Sandy, the Dachshund, but having a good time with Peanut, the Dorkie, after getting her homework checked. Around 6:15 p.m., Lillie told Lana she wanted to come in to see Sandy. Lana didn't want to open the door- afraid the puppy would run out, even though she checked frequently with me to see where she was. Once she let her in, she brought Peanut into the room also, and Delorean, Lillie's daughter came in a moment later. Lillie sat on the couch and played with Sandy and asked Lana what she thought Sandy was going to do to her. Lana- "I don't know. I'm just afraid of her." Then Lana sat between Lillie and I and Lillie plopped Sandy on Lana's lap. Instantly Lana started playing with her and spent the rest of the evening, even after her shower, playing with both dogs. It was fast and amazing.

Now, the dream.

I saw a barbershop with its light on and a couple of people inside and decided to stop in to get the back of my hair shaped up. As I got closer, there were 2 women barbers, and one male customer. I saw a sign that said the hours were 7 to 7 that day and asked if I was too late, because it was 7:15pm. The man turned his chair around and, it was Nick, from the old neighborhood. We spoke and smiled and the lady got back to finishing him up. The other lady, a short heavy lady, with a stylist jacket on like a lab coat, came to me and we walked outside and she showed me across the street to another barber shop that stayed open a little later. We walked and talked out front for a few minutes and she was very sweet and funny. I asked her if I could come in the next morning and she said they open at 5 a.m. on Saturdays and I would have to be there then because their regulars were going to be coming in and she thought it would be better. I said I would try my best to be there, but I would have to wake up my daughter which would be pretty *rough. We said good night and Nick got up to leave. He and I walked out together- through a hallway that led to what looked like the small lobby of an apartment building. Outside we walked and he asked me how much shoes cost or how many pairs of shoes I could get for $100. I said one or two, depending on the style and quality. He said something about wanting to do something for me and Lana because he knew me first, before his wife. I told him he really didn't have to give us anything but I appreciated the thought. It was getting darker and I don't know where we were going, but we walked the whole way and* I woke up thinking about my pre-teen and teenage years of infatuation with him. Strange. Then I thought about the ring dance and the kiss with Roger Jackson, another neighbor cutie. He told everybody that I couldn't kiss- actually, I was and still am a great kisser, but it was Roger. I wasn't interested in him, at all, so I couldn't fake a kiss. But, I had to prove myself so I went to his house a couple of days later just to show him. Cleared that rumor up.

I vaguely remember a kiss with Nick and if I'm remembering right, it wasn't bad at all, but it was such a long time ago.

Time to get back to today and get ready for work.

Motorcycle Traffic Jam, RHS Uniforms and Lost in RHS

September 14

Dear Dream Maker,

Going to be a quick write. I need to catch up on a few dreams. *On last Saturday night, I dreamed about riding with Patrice somewhere and we stopped at a light. There was a young Hispanic girl around 9 or 10 years old on the corner waiting to cross. She had on something white and a skirt with white and red, yellow, and green swirling designs. We turned, I think, but maybe the light took a long time and Patrice said, I knew I should have gone the other way. I told her that there are lights all over so it wouldn't have mattered. Our light changed, we turned, and there was some commotion in the street up ahead. People got out of their cars because traffic had stopped and we got out and saw several motorcycles- black all over, and the drivers wore blue, long-sleeved shirts under black vests with blue and white helmets. There were maybe 15 or 20 of them. They drove to a point and stopped and all of them got off of their motorcycles. Then a bunch of police cars came behind them and got out of cars with their dogs, mostly Shepherds.*

Strange thing- Sunday, I went riding on the highway on my motorcycle for the first time with George and his friend Manny and we went to a bike show- a continuation of the show Patrice and I took the puppies to the night before. There I saw three guys pull into the lot dressed just like my dream. They were with others, maybe 4 more, but those three made my mouth drop. Weird. *Yes, I will buy myself a motorcycle. That will be my graduation gift to myself.

Sunday night, *I dreamed I was at RHS and I went to an office to pick up uniforms. I was given a thick garment bag with BDUs in it. I haven't thought about Army life in several years, but I had my uniforms there. Then I saw me putting them in a shopping cart and rolling them toward my classroom, but it was 205 instead of 207. A few minutes later, I was returning to the quartermaster to get more. This time I got dress uniforms and BDUs, and my student Enya Cruz was walking with me. Even more strange.*

Last night, *I dreamed about being lost in RHS. The building was much larger and really a maze inside. I was in the lobby talking with someone and because time was getting short before my next class, I decided to take the stairs nearest me. I went up a flight and nothing looked familiar, even though it should have. I went up spiral stairs and through a few doors and short hallways. Bells rang and I didn't see any faces I recognized- very few people out at all. Then I realized I was 10 minutes late and called the office from my cell phone. I didn't tell Mrs. Benson that I was lost in the building but I asked her to page Mrs. Allen (science department chair) and have her call me. I turned around and tried to go back the way I had come and made it to the outside of the building and saw Mrs. Allen drive up. We walked in together and I told her what happened and I went to Mrs. Benson and told her and then went to class the way I knew to go.* Different.

Diary Entry

September 18

I don't recall my dreams from last night if there were any, but I just wanted to write a little before I get ready for school. I just haven't been able to sleep well too many nights. Saturday night I took half of a sleeping pill from my doctor and it made me feel so dizzy, I could barely stand about 45 minutes after I took it. I don't like that feeling. I guess I was supposed to be in bed waiting for it to kick in instead of folding laundry. Anyway, I slept through the night, until around 6 a.m.

Yesterday, I thought about my Dad a lot. I really miss him. I watched a little of Father of the Bride II and Steve Martin said to the doctor delivering the babies- "These two women are my life." I thought about the two most significant men in mine and they're not here anymore and just cried. I try not to get really caught up in missing them but sometimes it's just overwhelming.

Last night, I woke up a few times- no pill. I couldn't seem to make myself get into bed before 11 p.m. and I watched a little TV- some gory cartoon about a Barbarian. I woke up around 12:30 a.m., then after 2, then at 4:45, and just couldn't hold my bathroom need until the alarm so I'm up. Now it's 5:20 and I think I'm going to get dressed and set up Lana for breakfast before I take Peanut and Sandy outside.

During the night, I thought about the youth forensic detective's course I'm scheduled to teach starting next week. In my mind, I was setting up labs or picking different fingerprint activities to do. Maybe because the last thing I did before I got in bed was write out a bunch of things I want to order from Ward's for the class. I have to get the information to Mrs. Richardson, the project coordinator, this afternoon.

I guess I'd better get moving.

Dear Lord,

I thank you always for everything you do and have done for me and my daughter. She is truly a blessing and I love her very much. Please continue to help me take care of her. Please watch over and guide my friends and my family. We all need to be reminded of your strength and value and the feeling of peace you provide in our hurting moments and hours. I miss my Dad. Thank you for the hugs you send from him through Lana and others.

Thank you and I love you.

Crush Friends and Flooded

September 28

Dear Dream Maker,

As usual, I have to make it quick. *Last night I dreamed about the old neighborhood Nick. Somehow he was in a bedroom with me and I was telling him about dreams I had a few weeks ago with him as a main character. He told me that I could talk to him and even though he was married he still wanted a friendship with me or for me to be able to get in touch with him if I needed to. I was highly skeptical about that and he wanted to know why and said something about what I had told him about being his first wife. I think I blushed. He sat on the bed and then laid down and told me I could lay beside him. The bed was really soft and I felt like I was going to fall off but he held on to me and pulled me closer. The conversation continued but I was not where I should have been.* This just reconfirms that I can't call their house and talk with the Kirk family about anything personal. I do want to invite their girls for a sleepover in November.

I also had a dream where Sophia, my sister-in-law, came in rushing to go to a job interview or coming from one and we were in a basement with laundry. The washer had flooded the floor and there were wet towels down. We weren't surprised by the flooding- it was as if it were a regular thing for that space. All I remember is her asking me how I was doing and me answering in a not-too-excited way, "Kind of down."

I've decided that I'm going to lose weight. I'm not sure how yet but I will get up and exercise like I used to- just for a few minutes at first to get back into it then increase. I went over my mark and need to get back to the other side soon. I want to get a motorcycle and I don't want to look bad on one. I also need to find a hairstyle again. My short look is growing and I haven't been going to get it done as often as I used to so I need to get back to that too. I think I want to get it braided in the spring so I won't be cutting it down, just keeping the shape-up and ends trimmed.

Allergy time is kicking in. I had my sleep study last Saturday. I hope to hear something to settle my mind about my sleep habits. I already know that there won't be any more snacking after 9 p.m. now, but I realized a week ago that the snacks I have don't seem to make a difference in my dreaming or quality sleeping. I wake up with or without them.

Lord, please be a strength for me to get myself in shape. I know I want to be around for myself and for my daughter. I'm so very blessed and you have been a shoulder so often. I pray that I can reach my goal weight- I'm setting now, without much thought- 180 lbs. I don't know how to set a time for it, but I'll aim for Christmas or January 1. Thank you and please take care of my baby, my family, and my friend Brandon whom I love, as well as all of my friends. I pray for Lana's Uncle Mark and his situation and for my friend Shelby's family in their time of loss.

Thank you,
Tangie

Hula Dancing Meena

September 29
Dear Dream Maker,

Last night or this morning more likely, I dreamed about our family returning from a trip to Hawaii. Aunt Meena had us put on some music from there and she did a hula dance she learned. It looked really nice for a few minutes. She did smooth and graceful hand movements and looked good doing it. She wore a long dress, colorful, and she had on a lei and a flower in her hair. Toward the end of the dance, she took several steps back, bumping into an ironing board and a table, and fell backward. Her legs went up into the air as the table broke. Everyone rushed over to make sure she was alright and she laughed which made it okay for us to laugh. I was taping her performance and we decided to send it to America's Funniest Home Videos. The dance was played and replayed on the part where she fell backward. Aunt Angie, Grandma Tally, Aunt Bridgette, and a few others were there. I think they decided to have Aunt Meena go to the hospital to make sure she wasn't seriously injured.

We got in bed before 9:30 last night and I woke up around 1 a.m. because I heard the puppies fighting. I might need to put them in the cage at night to start getting them to go to the potty outside in the morning.

I miss my Brandon - his drama with the baby's mother continues and will continue here on out so I feel like I should let go of any hope for a better relationship with us. There's nothing I can do to help. I like having his friendship but what more can it be. Oh well.

The bike search continues and this weekend there are a couple of bike shows but I don't have anyone to keep Lana for me so I might need to forget about that. Maybe we can do the Smithsonian or the Sunday stunt show.

Diary Entry

October 5

I don't have dream information to record this morning. I just wanted to get a few things out of my head. I feel like I am losing my mind and am so overwhelmed with work and life in general for me is just rushed. Mid-week is hectic and I want to throw things, scream or kick something. My head hurts more these days and I want to take a nap. I pray and try to sit still then feel like I'm not getting enough done.

My grading pile is continuously growing and I have plenty I need to do at home too, but I just cannot get much done daily. I don't know what to do. Sitting down to write out a schedule for a few things just adds another thing to my long mental list of things to do. I just feel stressed and really don't have anything to be stressed over. I know that but can't seem to shake the feeling. I talked with my mom about it and she said I may need to get a weekend away. I would like to and wish I could spend time with Brandon as well but money is a little tight this week- trying to pay down everything and getting a second mortgage- equity loan to consolidate all of my credit cards and plan for my motorcycle. (Counterproductive. I know.) Maybe that's part of it. Or maybe it's Fulla's birth date coming up next week. I'm just not sure.

Last night after dance class, on the way to Burger King with Lana, she told me about some things she remembers about her dad. She said he was sick and he yelled a lot at that girl. She remembers them sleeping and her getting into bed with them. She remembered getting a pineapple from the refrigerator, sneaking.

I don't remember how the conversation came up. I told her a month or two ago that I would try harder not to yell and most of the time I've been doing good. I listen to her when she scolds the dogs and she sounds angry and I ask, who talks to you like that? She says, "No one." I don't know where that comes from, but I want that particular behavior to change. Overall, she's doing pretty good and growing beautifully. I love her so much.

Dear Lord,

Please help me through the blues and anxiety I have been feeling. I feel lost right now and overwhelmed. I miss happier moments. I am grateful for all I have been able to learn and do and now I'm just confused. Do I keep searching for a job? Do I add Maryland for a job search? Do I consider a doctorate? Am I giving Lana enough time? When do I get more grading done or do I need to change my style of work distribution? Why don't I sleep? What do my dreams mean?

Please give me the guidance I need to make good choices for myself and for Lana. Please take care of my friend Brandon - I love him and hope for the best for him and baby girl and all involved. Please take care of my Mother- she's always a shoulder for me and I love her so much. Please watch over Mark as he sorts out his issues. Thank you for my family and friends- I know they are there for me but it is difficult to call on some of them. Like many, I try to work out or sort out my issues and problems on my own or just by bringing them to God. Letting go of them is the hard part. I will try harder.

Thank you for all you have given me and today is a better day.

Amen.

The Babies

October 16

Dear Dream Maker,

I woke once last night around 4:45 a.m. I think I had already dreamed the first half. *I dreamed about Cheryl and her youngest son Jeff on Kenmore. They lived in the house next door to ours. Jeff was very young- around 5 or 6 years old and he was slow. I talked to him for a few minutes and heard it in his voice and in what he was saying- as if he belonged in preschool. My mom had said something about him to me and she was there, too. Then we were in a house across the street and sitting and talking in a living room. It was kind of dim- sunlight only. Cheryl was sitting on the end of a couch and holding a baby. The baby was on the lighter side of the brown spectrum with a lot of hair. She was drinking from a bottle, trying to hold it but not quite strong enough to keep it steady herself. When she was done drinking,*

Pedina (yes, Pedina, another neighbor from Kenmore) picked up the baby and started talking to her and playing with her. I think the baby was hers. Cheryl told her, "That's why she throws up as soon as you get her. She's not ready to be tossed around right after she eats."

Somewhere I recall talking to Wilson Gundy, the discipline dean at RHS, about getting barriers with ropes for the Haunted Hall my forensic club held.

Then I was at an ice-skating show. Mikail Baryshnikov and another man were performing together. It was graceful and nice. When they finished, they went to seats in a box near the floor. I, for some reason, went over and sat with them. In the box were the two skaters, in street clothes, and another big guy- white with a receding hairline and thick curly dark hair. There was the baby, too. She was in a carrier drinking from a bottle, just looking around. The big guy spoke to me and asked me something about where I was from or where I worked and then commented that maybe I could have said or done something about his girlfriend. They had just broken up and he wasn't sure why. He was talking about Patrice. Somewhere in my dreams I had already seen and talked with this guy about his girlfriend. I talked with the group and asked if I could hold the baby and they let me. Strange combination of recollections.

I'm getting myself stressed again- anticipation- the haunted hall set-up, the money, the loan, Mom and Aunt Angie coming up to visit, Auntie K and Cousin Leon's mess, being lonely, not finishing my school grading, the Tuesday night kids forensics class, wanting to write my book, not exercising enough, having a messy house, wanting to move, wanting another job, not have my degree paperwork- a lot of things I need to just give to God.

Dear Lord,

I thank you for always listening to my pitiful cries and knowing my needs. Please be with me today through my classroom observation and through all those things I seem to carry with no need. It's all yours- you know the outcome and I know only that I have nothing to worry about. Thank you for my little princess and for all of my family and friends. Please continue to watch over us all.

I love you
I miss my Dad. Please hug him for me.

Short Bus Ride

October 26, 9:40 p.m.

I'm very tired- it's been one of those weeks- getting ready for the haunted hall and for Mom and Aunt Angie coming into town. I wanted to put down my dream from last night. My sleep is still jacked up.

The dream: *I saw a bus- like a double-decker trolley on the inside and an MTA (Mass Transit Administration) on the outside. There were about 50 people on it, and it had stopped on the street where a lot of dancing and music was going on. A few more people got on and the driver stepped down from his seat and said he was going downstairs for a few minutes. He walked down what looked like steps into a lower level of the bus.*

Jefferson Memorial Hospital

November 12

Even though my notebook has been sitting very near my bed for weeks, I haven't thought much about writing. I did feel like it was important this morning though.

Last night, I bought my motorcycle. It's nice-a blue and white Yamaha YZF 600R. I'm excited but I made a promise to Brother Willie and to myself to take my time.

Still missing my Brandon. *He showed up in a dream last night. I had to go in his drawer for something-underwear, I think. I broke the drawer and put it in backward. The room was in our (his and mine) house. I don't remember anything else yet.*

Mom and Aunt Angie were here from October 27th to November 7th. Mom and I went to Philadelphia with Aunt Estelle, Uncle Richard, Cousin Alissa and her boys, and took my girl to the memorial service at Jefferson University Hospital. The service was very sweet and positive. There were a lot of families there and about 25 or more names were read. I missed Dad openly- I will always think of when he said "Make good choices" and smiled. That was our inside joke.

Dear Lord,

Please kiss my daddy's cheek for me. I miss him so much. I wish I could show him our puppies, my new car, and now my motorcycle. Lord bless my decisions- give me guidance and clarity of thought. Help me to be a good mother and raise my beautiful gift, my girl Lana. Thank you. Please take care of my mom and my family, my brother especially, and my friends. Thank you.

Lovingly, Tangela

Has a dream ever influenced your decision or plan? What was the outcome?
Was your dream a good influence to the decision or plan?

_____
_____
_____
_____
_____
_____
_____
_____
_____
_____
_____
_____
_____
_____
_____
_____
_____
_____
_____
_____
_____
_____
_____
_____
_____
_____
_____

John Legend, Corbin Bleu, and All My Children

December 11, 5:39 a.m.
    14 days until Christmas.

It took me several minutes to decide whether to get up and type my dream since I haven't been doing it lately. Then it dawned on me that my journal is right here in front of me.

I have recently dreamed about John Legend- looking crazy with shaved sideburns, a Jerry curl, and a ponytail. We had met before then and I went to see him after a concert. I figured that it must be time to open and listen to his CD that I bought over a month ago.

Last week sometime, I dreamed about Corbin Bleu (a Disney channel actor), a really cute young man. He wanted to date me, but he was too young. I had cooked or was cooking dinner and he said something about rice with vinegar and he made it. I think it was good. I asked him how old he was, and he said in a deep voice, "37" and I just laughed, and we talked more.

Last night I dreamed I had taken my chil<u>dren</u> to the doctor. I have three older boys (older teens) and Lana and a few other young ones. Who the father was, I don't know. After their examinations, I met one son, Darius Brody, in a room to make sure everything was OK and talked with him about getting a girl pregnant and about marriage. Weird. *Also, the office people kept talking about the girl who was out that day-CZ. Cheryl something. I got in a line to pay for whatever I was getting. A lot of people were ahead of me- maybe 8 to 10. I saw the guy from Girlfriends (TV show), Raheem, and we spoke- we had done a show or something together before.*

There was another one about me riding my bike on Friday night but it's 5:51 a.m. and time to get it together.

Just Writing...Sam Cooke Play, Me and My Premonitions and Thankfulness

December 18,

Dear Dream Maker,

It's been a while since I took the time to write my thoughts down. I don't have much time in the mornings, like now.

This weekend was decent for the most part except for a scare with my mother. First off, I went to a play- *Sam Cooke, Forever, Mr. Soul*, with Aunt Neona, Vonda, and Patrice. The play was great and the actor was very attractive. My Music guy friend, a lifelong pen pal, was the music director for it and invited us to come to Delaware for the play and for dinner. It was truly wonderful to see him again after 20 years. He's such a nice person. On the way home I checked messages and found out that my mother had gone to the hospital because she felt weird. She hadn't eaten all day but found out that everything was at the right levels- blood, sugar, etc. She had gone and gotten home by the time we went to the play and were heading home. It didn't truly hit me until I had gotten everyone else home and got in my own room, and then I cried for a while. I miss my Dad so much and I really don't want to lose my mother too. I talked with her a few times, and she is being watched over by Ms. Blossom, her boarder/ friend, and a few others, so I'm glad she isn't alone.

When I talked with Mom, I mentioned my angels that watch out for her, and she reminded me of the premonition I had shared with her earlier this month. A voice told me- "Tangie, something is not right with your mom. Come on down." It was around 5:30-5:45 a.m. and I called her at her job to make sure she was okay. She said she felt fine. She must have called a few people shortly afterward because they called me to make sure **I** was okay. Probably not.

We are heading to Florida on Sunday for Christmas. I'm ready for the change of scenery even if it's just for a week.

Yesterday, I got a lot of little cleaning done- my room, some living room stuff, and laundry. I went out on my motorcycle around the neighborhood and it felt great. When I got home to put it away, I had some trouble and had to lay it down. It took a lot of strength to get it back up, but thanks to God, I got it upright. Then I couldn't get it back into the garage, because I needed a push to go up that incline in front of the garage. I asked my neighbor right behind me and she helped. I cracked myself up doing all that. I did hurt my left wrist- which I'm feeling now.

Lana was in a play yesterday afternoon at Cousin Teresa and Rodney's church. The play was nice and everyone involved did a great job. I am very proud of my little girl. Besides being spoiled and sometimes selfish, she's a good kid and I love her so much.

She mentioned on a classwork assignment that she wants a Dad for Christmas. When I read it, the tears just flowed. She is doing very well with her reading also. It's exciting to hear her ask me to listen to her spell or to read different things.

Lord, thank you for letting my Mother be okay. Please take care of her. Thank you for my little girl and please help me to take care of her. Thank you for all of those who are helping care for my Mother and me. Thank you for allowing me to fall down and get back up yesterday. I appreciate the machine I bought better now. Thank you for the trip to Delaware to see a dear friend. I love him and learn so much from him- the importance of keeping in touch. I love you for being available to me to listen and hear my cries and sorrows and to be encouraging so that they don't last too long. I love you for the exciting times you provide so that I can know that all we do is not in vain and that there are reasons to be happy and content. Thank you.

Names

Tangela Renae Mason Carper
Lenore Mason
Franklin Mason
Davison/Davi Mason
Sophia Mason
Aunt Neona (new moon) Simpson
Monique
Jeannette (Monique's mom)
Vonda Simpson
Uncle Louis Mason
Aunt Rose/Rosette Bridges
Auntie K/Yvonne Young
Hazel Maxwell (Bibi)
Uncle Derrick Bowden
Uncle Richard Mason
Sophia Vinnie Bowden
Uncle Charles Bowden
Aunt Sarah Bowden
Amara Bowden Grant
Aunt Estelle Stanley
Aunt Eva Parker
Scarlet Cook
Cynthia Bowden Barrett
Noelle Simpson
Leon Paxton
Mike/Michael Bowden (Bird)
Greg Carter
Grace Carter
Mason Family
Deana McKinley
Emmanuel McKinley
Shelby Bell
Joseph Bell
Angie/Angela Bowden
Adam Bowden
Nina Bowden
Keith Bowden
Cyres Simpson
Naomi
Benton Spears
Copeland Family
Aunt Regina
Candace
Whitney
Alissa Haven
Keith Haven
Kevin Haven

Tammy Copeland
Bridgette Liston
Wendell Warren
Philameena Bowden
Tally Bowden
Ms. Blossom
Harmony
Fulla/Fuller Carper, Jr.
Adrienne
Cassia Thorn
Fuller Carper
Veronica Carper
Mark Chale
Margot
Uncle Ronald
Maureen
Rome
Roland
Sylvia
Serena
Penny
Damien Douglas
Marcus (Rome's brother)
Donis
Ms. Elizabeth

Neighborhood Friends
Nicholas/Nick Kirk
Joyce
Brissa
Nigel Clark
Damon Townes
Elliott Jenkins
Camilla Jenkins
Robbie Jenkins
Curtis Shepherd
Patrick Briggs
Kenja Griffin
Steve Roundhill
Deloreon Knox
Lillie Knox
Roger Jackson
Cheryl Brown
Jeff Brown
Pedina
Friends
Hannah (flower)
Elayne Bolton Durande

Kama Duponte
Paul, Jr. (Elayne's son)
Kalie (beloved)
Tyler Family
Ava Tyler Bianco
Annette Tyler (Ava's sister)
Mavis Tyler (Ava's mom)
*Gabriel Davis
Patrice Hatton
Lurena Brown Bennett
*Brandon Russell
Dana Sanders
Dr. Ruby Smith
Cody
Bishop Miner
Harold Green
Phaedra
April
Trey
Ortega Family
Tiff

Coworker Friends
Leona Wiley
Rick Stephens
Jack Miller
Ms. Tice (silent)
Rod/Rodney Torres
Dr. Norman
Katherine
Jawad Abdullah
Chris Foster
Ashleigh Richardson
Dean Brooks
Ms. Haven
Kenneth
Jarrett Windsor
Dept. Chair Erica Allen
Omar Scott
Jonathan Camar
Mr. Martin
Lt. Marshall
Spence Rosen
Zara Snow
Ms. Combs
Katrina Cooper
Mrs. Benson
Mrs. Richardson

Wilson Gundy
Valeria Watts
Timothy
*Jason Monroe
Lorece Fenlon
Rona Saunders
Saree
Marvin Edwards
Diane Edwards
Thomas Coles
Maya Franklin
Mr. Andrews
Olive Stephens
Ren
Min. Paul Phillips
Rev. Owens
Ofc. Bx
Stephanie
Enya
Alex
Miss Dara
Sharon Wade
Charlotte Granger
Shannon Townsend
Pastor Crowder
Ms. Wilkenson
Mrs. Butler
Dina Butler
Pamela Butler
Austin Owens
Melanie Parker
Angelique Campbell
Francine Graham
Dr. Jean-Baptiste
Cathy Phillips
Carla Jackson
Ms. Connie
Tobias Nolan
Vincent Nolan
Dr. Stein
Duane
Stanley Johnson
Brandon Short
Terrance Ellis
Terrence Kemp
Enya Cruz
George